Arthur Schüller: Founder of Neuroradiology

A Life on Two Continents

Arthur Schüller: Founder of Neuroradiology

A LIFE ON TWO CONTINENTS

JOHN KEITH HENDERSON
WITH MICHAEL A HENDERSON

HYBRID
PUBLISHERS

Published by Hybrid Publishers

Melbourne Victoria Australia

© Michael Henderson 2021

This publication is copyright. Apart from any use
as permitted under the Copyright Act 1968, no part may be reproduced
by any process without prior written permission from the publisher.
Requests and inquiries concerning reproduction should be addressed to
the Publisher, Hybrid Publishers,
PO Box 52, Ormond, Victoria, Australia 3204.

www.hybridpublishers.com.au

First published 2021

A catalogue record for this
book is available from the
National Library of Australia

NATIONAL LIBRARY OF AUSTRALIA

ISBN: 9781925736601 (p)
9781925736618 (e)

Cover design: Gittus Graphics
Typeset in Adobe Garamond Pro
Printed in Australia by McPherson's Printing Group

All the photos included in this book come from the Schüller Archive, except for
those on pages 18 and 19, taken by Andrew Schuller; page 89 courtesy of Australian
National Archives; page 118 courtesy of the Archives and Heritage Centre, St
Vincent's Hospital Melbourne; and page 164, provided by Patricia Austen (Schüller
Archive).

Contents

Keith Henderson never got around to writing a dedication
for his work.

There is absolutely no doubt that the first person he would wish to
dedicate this work to was his beloved wife of nearly sixty-five years,
Marguerita (known to all as Pixie) Leo Doyle.

Cor ad Cor Loquitor
Heart speaks unto heart.
– JH Newman

This book is also dedicated to the memory of my father's friend, mentor
and colleague, Arthur Schüller, his wife and family.

Finally he would also want to dedicate this book to the memory of the
people who cared for the Schüllers during their time in Australia. Their
humanity and decency stands in stark contrast
to what the Schüllers experienced in their native land.

John Keith Henderson

Foreword

As best as can be determined, my father, Keith Henderson, started his research on the life of Arthur Schüller in the late 1980s shortly after he formally retired as head of the Department of Neurosurgery at St Vincent's Hospital Melbourne; however, he had been clearly thinking about it and accumulating material for years prior to this. His work was methodical and slow. It was frequently interrupted, particularly by the ill-health of his wife Pixie and occasionally by other family matters.

He was always a great reader, particularly of history, but sensibly he took the wise move of reading how to write biography and history at an early stage in the writing of this manuscript. This was fairly typical behaviour for my father who loved both reading and books but, more importantly, accumulating knowledge and understanding of his world. The end result was a large amount of well-organised information.

When Arthur Schüller walked out unannounced from the Radiology Department at St Vincent's Hospital in 1956 for the last time, he left behind very little of his own notes but most of his books. Frank Morgan arranged for these items to be stored in the Neurosurgery Department and years later, simply by my father's fiat, they became the Schüller Archive. It contains many books from the early years of neuroradiology, including of course Schüller's own works and many of his published papers, but little else.

My father added materially to this collection, which now includes details of interviews with people who knew Schüller and any records, documents etc. he was able to procure in the course of his investigations. These are detailed in the Appendix. Many of these investigations came to naught, given the passage of time and the destruction of Austrian infrastructure during the war. Schüller kept virtually no correspondence, and what little we have from him is almost entirely of a professional nature. As became clear during editing of this work, many of the incidents in Schüller's life described here were recounted to my father by Schüller himself.

It appears that the bulk of what my father wrote was completed at least five years prior to his death in 2017. His mind was still active, but due to increasing frailty it was a major effort to do anything more than tinker around the edges of his manuscript. My father and I had many discussions about this book, as well as life in Oxford in the 1950s, and his time at St Vincent's Hospital, all of which were valuable in my role as editor.

In editing this work I have tried to remain true to his original conception. There has been some minor editing in moving sections, particularly in the first three chapters, to suit the flow of the narrative, and one chapter which was small has been deleted, but the material was incorporated into chapters 3 and 4. Minor grammatical errors, which were fortunately infrequent, have been rectified and a few details clarified, particularly dates, where they were missing or ambiguous.

A small amount of material has been added, for the most part based on material my father had collected and preserved in the Schüller Archive. These additions have been incorporated to either improve the flow of the narrative, clarify points raised in the narrative or seemed to the editor to be sufficiently important to be included.

As detailed below, a number of my father's colleagues and family reviewed the penultimate manuscript. Based on their comments, further information where it was available or clarification of specific issues was undertaken. A small amount of background material relating to general medical, political or social matters has been added to explain or clarify critical events during Schüller's life. A small amount of additional information was gathered from my father's circle and from other sources. Further information has come to light in recent years, including a record of Arthur and Grete's baptism and renunciation of the Jewish religion; details of Grete's will have also been included.

One chapter, "In Illo Tempore", has not been materially altered. It describes the fate of Grete's mother and Arthur and Grete's two sons, daughter-in-law and granddaughter at the hands of the Nazis. It is a devastating piece of writing. It is a tribute to my father and in no way could I improve it. At times his prose could be a little flowery but the writing in this chapter is lucid, quiet, and simple; the stark nature of its presentation contrasts with the obscenity of the fate of these people. Because he told me many times, I know the information on which he based this chapter had a major impact on his appreciation and understanding of Arthur Schüller.

By circumstance, during the early years of research for this volume, my father had the great fortune to make contact with Erwin Schindler, who was at that time Professor of Neuroradiology in the University of Vienna, and who was also deeply interested in the life of Arthur Schüller. They corresponded and exchanged information, ideas and encouragement.

In 2000, Erwin and his wife, Karen, were on an overseas holiday and specifically came to Melbourne to meet with Keith, who was unable to travel, having taken on the care of his wife Pixie. My father was very grateful for the assistance of Erwin and it was always his view that this volume would be a joint effort. There is no doubt, as my father would testify, that Erwin's contribution was significant. Schindler died unexpectedly in 2003 and never saw the fruits of their work.

A number of other people contributed in significant ways to this book. There will be some of whom I remain unaware and I express my apologies to them. The foremost to acknowledge is one of my father's dearest friends, Tom King FRCS, FRACS. Tom provided many articles and assisted materially in chasing down information on Schüller's time in Oxford. More important was his companionship and wise counsel. Similar comments can be made for many of Keith's other dear friends, including Bob Southby FRACS, Peter McNeil FRACS and Donald Simpson FRACS.

Finally, I must acknowledge Andrew Schuller, who by the most extraordinary of circumstances came to this project. An old friend from Keith's Oxford days, John Potter FRCS who was helping Keith with Schuller's Oxford days, asked his neighbour named Schuller if he knew anything about his namesake. The neighbour, who was Andrew's father, didn't know anything about Arthur but by this time his son Andrew, who was researching the family, learned of Keith's interest from contacts in Brno, and he initiated contact. Simultaneously a friend of the Schindlers in Melbourne who was aware of Andrew's interest brought them together. Andrew, a publisher, is Arthur Schüller's great-nephew. I thank them all for their friendship and assistance to my father.

Although I take responsibility for any omissions or other mistakes, I wish to acknowledge many of the above who read the manuscript and provided me with many comments, suggestions and corrections. I would especially like to thank my brother John, sister Tina, and my daughter Catherine, who willingly assisted in the editing of this manuscript.

Michael A Henderson, 1 December 2020
e: Michael.Henderson@petermac.org

Erwin Schindler

Introduction

For as long as I can remember there was always a picture in my father's study of an elderly man with a shock of white hair. At the base of the photograph was a signature: it was Arthur Schüller's. I am not sure that my father could remember when he first decided to write his old mentor's biography. After the initial flurry of tributes following Schüller's death, nothing of any substance concerning his life and place in modern neuroradiology was published until the works of Keith Henderson, my father, and Erwin Schindler in the late 1990s.

My father died at the age of ninety-four in 2017, and as his oldest child and the only doctor in the family, both of us had tacitly agreed previously that I would see this project through. We often spoke of the book and, despite many offers of assistance, he wished to remain in control even as he became increasingly frail. It was as if finishing the book would mean the finish of him, and although this was unsaid between us, we both respected each other's position. Many of our discussions in retrospect were obviously for my benefit.

As is not made entirely clear in his manuscript, his association with Schüller goes back to his time as a trainee in Frank Morgan's neurosurgical unit at St Vincent's Hospital, Melbourne, between 1946 and 1950, and as a junior consultant neurosurgeon from 1954 to 1956. As the surgical trainee, he met with Schüller on a daily basis in the x-ray department, the neurosurgical ward and the operating room.

My father and Schüller shared a love of classical music; both were shy, and both cared deeply for people. It was clear in listening to my father in recent years that they had more than a professional relationship, and indeed Arthur Schüller and his wife attended my parents' wedding in November 1950. Nevertheless, there was always a sense that Schüller was the master and my father the student; there were certain boundaries that should not be breached. My father told me on more than one occasion that Schüller never discussed the appalling tragedy of his family, or other personal matters, with him or anyone else, except perhaps Frank Morgan.

Schüller was remembered in Vienna as a gifted teacher and similarly he was a recognised figure around St Vincent's Hospital Melbourne. It is not often remembered, but Schüller trained initially as a psychiatrist and neurologist before he became the founder of neuroradiology, but he was also a scientist and a clinician, and in 1940s Melbourne, he was a phenomenon that went largely unrecognised.

I have, of course, to confess my bias, but in listening to my father, I sensed that Schüller found someone in him who shared his passion for learning. My father knew as much neuroradiology as many neuroradiologists, and could compete on an almost equal footing with the neuropathologists. He was regarded around Melbourne for many years as providing one of the best neurological opinions in town, despite the fact he was a surgeon.

In retrospect, it is now obvious how profound an influence Schüller had on my father's training and career. Ostensibly, this is why Keith wrote this biography. But there is more to this story that unfolded over the years of his research into Schüller's life. As Keith better understood the chronic and corrosive effects of anti-Semitism, and the obscenity of national socialism and the Final Solution, he came to better understand their impact on the life of his mentor and friend, and the whole Schüller family. There was a personal dimension that this recognition brought for him that demanded a response.

Timeline

1874, 28 December: Born Brünn / Brno, Moravia now Czech Republic.

1894, August: commences medical training, University of Vienna.

1899, November: Graduated in Medicine University of Vienna, awarded Franz Joseph Prize, "sub auspiciis Imperatoris Francesci Josephi" for the perfect mark.

1900: Medical residency Franz-Joseph Ambulatorium.

1901: Research program Professor A Munk Berlin Berlin.

1902: Assistant Physician to Professor Emil Redlich in the neurology clinic at the Children's Hospital Vienna.

1902: Joins Guido Holzknecht in the Central Roentgen Laboratory and remains as Honorary Research Fellow till 1938.

1902: Commences radiological study of the skull.

1904, March: Completes Neurology and Psychiatry training and is appointed Assistant in the Second Psychiatric Clinic, General Hospital (Allgemeine Krankenhaus), Vienna.

1904: Appointed Privat Docent, University of Vienna ("teacher").

1905: Early x-ray machine in his private consulting rooms.

1905: *The Skull Base on the Radiogram* published.

1906, December: Married Margarete Stiassni.

1907: Achieved Habilitiert fur Neurologie und Psychiatrie (formal recognition of research excellence following a dissertation).

1907: Appointed Venia Docendi (university lecturer).

1908: Arthur and Grete baptised Catholics.

1908: Franz born.

1909: Hans born.

1912: *Rontgen Diagnosis of Diseases of the Head* published.

1914: Schüller uses the term Neuro-Rontgenologie or Neuro-radiology for the first time in a general lecture.

1914: Appointed Professor, University of Vienna.

1915: Describes radiological appearances of what became known as Hand Schüller Christian Disease.

1938, 12 March: Germany annexes Austria (Anschluss).

1938: Nuremberg Laws enforced (limiting the rights and activities of Jewish people).

1938, 9-10 November: Black Thursday or *Kristallnacht*, "spontaneous" organised assaults on Jewish persons and properties throughout Germany and Austria particularly Vienna. Arthur was assaulted.

1939: Arthur and Grete leave Vienna forever for Oxford and is welcomed into the Nuffield Institute for Medical Research.

1939, 23 July: The Schüllers left Oxford for Antwerp to attend the first Symposium Neuroradiologicum, 24-28 July and then travelled to Australia.

1939, August: Arrived in Australia and shortly after commenced work in the Radiology Department and Neurosurgical Unit at, St Vincent's Hospital Melbourne.

1941: Honorary appointment University of Melbourne Department of Anatomy (formally confirmed 1 July 1945).

1941: Registered with the Commonwealth Alien Doctors Board.

1942: Registered with the Medical Board of New South Wales.

1945: "Naturalised" Australian citizen (and renunciation of Austrian citizenship).

1946: Registered with the Medical Board of Victoria.

1947: Elected to membership of the Neurosurgical Society of Australia.

1949, September: Honorary President of the Symposium Neuroradiologicum Rotterdam (did not attend).

1950, June: Schüllers buy No 2 Mortimer St, Heidelberg.

1956, 9 October:Last day working at St Vincent's Hospital.

1957, 31 October: Arthur Schüller died, St Vincent's Hospital Melbourne.

1972, 27 February: Grete Schüller died, St Vincent's Hospital Melbourne.

Schüller Family Tree

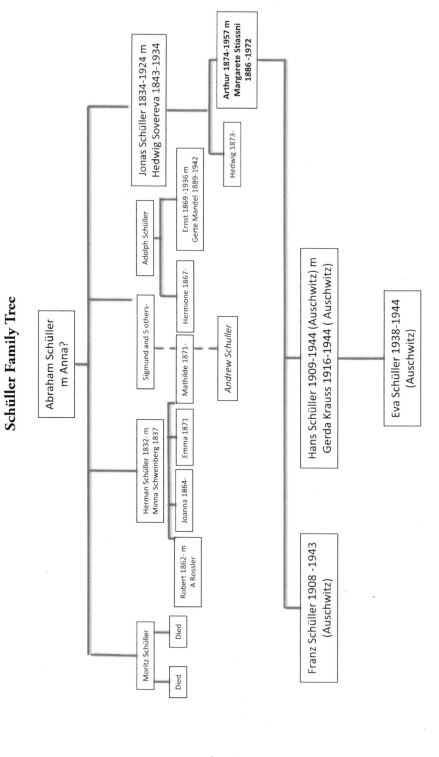

Abraham Schüller
m Anna?

Jonas Schüller 1834-1924 m
Hedwig Sovereva 1843-1934

Herman Schüller 1832- m
Minna Schweinberg 1837

Moritz Schüller

Adolph Schüller

Sigmund and 5 others-

Robert 1862- m
A Rossler

Joanna 1864-

Emma 1871

Mathilde 1871-

Hermione 1867-

Ernst 1869 -1936 m
Gerte Mandel 1889-1942

Hedwig 1873-

Arthur 1874-1957 m
Margarete Stiassni
1886 -1972

Andrew Schuller

Died

Died

Franz Schüller 1908 -1943
(Auschwitz)

Hans Schüller 1909-1944 (Auschwitz) m
Gerda Krauss 1916-1944 (Auschwitz)

Eva Schüller 1938-1944
(Auschwitz)

Stiassni Family Tree

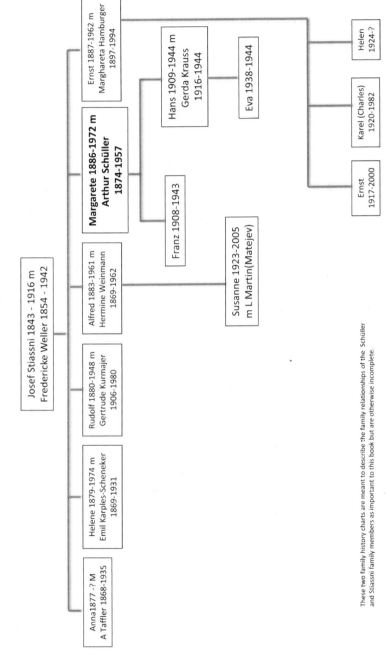

Josef Stiassni 1843 - 1916 m
Fredericke Weller 1854 - 1942

Anna 1877 -? M
A Taffler 1868-1935

Helene 1879-1974 m
Emil Karples-Scheneker
1869-1931

Rudolf 1880-1948 m
Gertrude Kurmajer
1906-1980

Alfred 1883-1961 m
Hermine Weinmann
1869-1962

**Margarete 1886-1972 m
Arthur Schüller
1874-1957**

Ernst 1887-1962 m
Marghareta Hamburger
1897-1994

Susanne 1923-2005
m L Martin(Matejev)

Franz 1908-1943

Hans 1909-1944 m
Gerda Krauss
1916-1944

Eva 1938-1944

Ernst
1917-2000

Karel (Charles)
1920-1982

Helen
1924-?

These two family history charts are meant to describe the family relationships of the Schüller and Stiassni family members as important to this book but are otherwise incomplete.

Chapter One

Origins – Fin de Siècle

Arthur Schüller was born on 28 December 1874 in Brünn/Brno in the Moravia region of the Austro-Hungarian Empire of Franz Joseph. (Brünn is the German name of the city; Brno is the Czech name, similarly, the name of the region is Mähren in German and Morava in Czech.)

As a young man he moved to Vienna for his undergraduate and postgraduate medical training at the University of Vienna Medical School. He remained attached to the university as a clinician, researcher and teacher until forced to leave his homeland in 1938 as a consequence of the annexation of Austria by Hitler's Germany. Arthur Schüller was, therefore, just as much a citizen of Austria as were the residents of Vienna where he spent most of his adult life.

He and his wife, with what few possessions they were permitted to retain, moved to Melbourne in 1939 and remained there till his death on 31 October 1957.

He was an extraordinarily intelligent and motivated individual who rose to the top of his chosen profession during some of the most tumultuous of times. He was the first person to systematically catalogue and describe the radiological appearances of the skull, and in due course his work led to the founding of the modern discipline of neuroradiology.

His life was marred by terrible tragedy, both personally and professionally, but those who remembered him, particularly during his time in Australia, did so with great fondness. He was remembered as a delightful and courteous but shy gentleman, though one who increasingly with the passage of time bore the weight of the world on his shoulders.

Arthur Schüller was the younger of two children born to Jonas Schüller and Hedwig Sovereva in Brno. Schüller's family can be traced back to his grandfather, Abraham Schüller, in the small rural town of Bučovice, about 40 km south east of Brno, now located in the Czech Republic.

The family lived in the Jewish ghetto located in the middle of town and were buried in the Jewish cemetery. The family was known to have manufactured alcohol and run a brewery. By the early nineteenth century, Abraham Schüller (1810–92), reputed among the family as a self-made man, took up weaving and by mid-century had established a small textile business. He expanded the business and moved to Brno, then a centre for the textile industry, where he prospered and became a wealthy man. Some of this wealth, further extended by his own father, passed down to Arthur.

Jonas was a specialist in diseases of the ear, nose and throat and a graduate of the Vienna Medical School. He trained in his specialty under Adam Politzer, one of the founders of the discipline and director of the first otology clinic in a medical school in the world. Jonas lived and practised in a house in the old Town Square of Brno, which still displays its early charm.

The Schüllers were ethnically Jewish, as was Arthur's mother's family, and Arthur certainly saw himself in this light. Both of Arthur's parents were buried in the Jewish cemetery in Brno.

Jewish people were recorded as living in Moravia by the second or third century CE, having followed the Roman armies up the Danube, providing various support services for the Legions. At the time of

Arthur's birth, the Austro-Hungarian Empire occupied a broad irregular zone extending from the Baltic Sea to the Adriatic where, for centuries, the German peoples in the West had pressed eastwards against the Slavs. The wide fault line between them included Bohemia and Moravia, which was now but a relic of the Kingdom of Great Moravia of a thousand years before, when it had occupied much of the territory later covered by the Austro-Hungarian Empire. Among the communities of this fault zone there were Jewish people, again with some division on an East–West basis.

In the middle of the eighteenth century Jewish people were largely excluded from Austria, in particular Vienna, and not for the first time. Over the centuries there had been many times when they were excluded from the city, usually because of blame for some natural disaster, the Black Death being a case in point. On one occasion the Empress blamed their presence in Vienna for her miscarriage and out they went again. Jewish people were denied careers in industry, commerce and banking, and the only profession open to them was medicine, but they were permitted to treat only Jewish patients. They were not eligible for service at Court, they were excluded from most areas of public service and could not rise high in the ranks of the military.

All of this began to improve after the reformist Emperor Joseph II introduced the Toleration Patent of 1782. Now Jewish people had access to public schools and the right to set up their own schools if they so desired; they could now aim for careers in commerce, industry and banking. The Emperor also thought that this would make the Jewish people "more useful to the State", a vision both pragmatic and prophetic. Nevertheless, anti-Semitism remained serious in Vienna, with periodic exacerbations as Jewish people migrated in increasing numbers into the city during the second half of the nineteenth century under the protective gaze of the Emperor. The last ghetto in Vienna closed with the ascent of Franz Joseph to the throne in 1848.

In the words of one historian, the Jews were now elevated to the status of "fully fledged second-class citizens".

❦

In nineteenth century Moravia there were tensions between the majority Czech population on the one hand and the minority Germans and the Hapsburg State on the other, aggravated by the Emperor declaring German to be the official language of the subject countries in the middle of the nineteenth century. Many people on both sides refused to use the language of the other in dealing with officialdom despite mingling personally in day-to-day harmony. The political and nationalistic differences notwithstanding, the citizens seem to have lived without personal strife for the most part. Friendships, work associations, sharing of a common culture and neighbourliness held the Moravian community together, yet Arthur Schüller never learnt to speak Czech, or so he claimed. Early in the nineteenth century anti-Semitism was relatively mild and mostly a matter of religious difference; but racial anti-Semitism was on the horizon and destined to become a serious problem, at least in Vienna, as the century proceeded.

❦

Jewish people in Moravia and Bohemia generally saw themselves as German, and were thus a minority group within the German-speaking minority. This group of German speakers, who lived in what was subsequently known to the world as the Sudetenland, would become the "justification" for Hitler to commence the invasion of Europe. This was the milieu into which Schüller was born.

His early years occurred during a progressively improving world for the Jewish people in the Austro-Hungarian Empire and without doubt provided him with the opportunities that facilitated his rise to international success. He was reared in a comfortable middle-class household, but beyond that we have no knowledge of his early years. There was an elder sister, Hedwige, born two years earlier, about whom nothing can now can be found.

His primary school years (*Volkschule*) could have been spent in a specifically Jewish school or in the government education system. In the latter case, he might have had some exposure to the Catholicism of his later life; the government had placed schools under the supervision of the Church so that some of the secular teaching was done by members of religious orders. In other schools the State paid priests to teach religion.

It is known that his secondary education was in the German language grammar school (*Gymnasium*) in Brno. Arthur excelled at school and was usually at the top of the class. He liked to point out that this included excellence in music: he was a fine violinist. Taken with his lifelong interest in Latin, this suggests that his secondary education was in the classical stream; he told his friend Frank Morgan that he always gained honours in art and the humanities. High school ended with success in the examination for the *Matura*, which qualified him for admission to any university in Germany or Austria.

Brno, even in the nineteenth century, was an ancient and historic centre which dominated southern Moravia. By then it had developed into an industrial centre, including a burgeoning textile industry which had probably encouraged the Schüller family to relocate there. The city had an excellent technical college but no university or medical school; this did not come about until the establishment of Masaryk University after the Second World War.

As a consequence, it was in Vienna that Arthur Schüller entered medical school in August 1894. He was no stranger to Vienna; the family was accustomed to move back and forth between the two cities, mainly for cultural events. Their financial situation ensured that he would be comfortably housed at a time when there was a housing crisis in Vienna, particularly for students with little money.

In the late nineteenth century there had been a considerable increase in population due to movement from the east, mainly from Galicia (a region straddling the modern border of Poland and the Ukraine). With such a housing shortage, like the native Viennese working class, many poorer students found themselves sharing a bed on a roster system. Most of them had to work for survival, a difficulty which Arthur was spared. In the late 1880s and the early 1890s the sight of the poor Jewish students, forced to earn a living, peddling their wares on the streets, led Theodor Billroth, the Professor of Surgery in the Second Clinic, to believe they were neglecting their studies for the sake of commercial advancement. He criticised this practice publicly and thus exposed himself to the allegation of anti-Semitism. Later, appreciating the true situation, he withdrew this criticism but his reputation took some time to recover.

Arthur Schüller had little, if any, contact with Billroth before he retired in 1894 (around the time Schüller entered the university) but he had stories to tell of an almost legendary figure. In later life he spoke approvingly of Billroth as a great surgical scientist and he did not raise the anti-Semitic issue against him. There is some evidence that years later Schüller was a member of a committee at the General Hospital that organised a statue of Billroth which still exists.

The move to Vienna for such a talented student was an entirely natural progression. The Vienna Medical School, then one of the most prestigious institutes in the world, was open to Franz Joseph's subjects. Just as enticing to a young man, Vienna at the turn of the twentieth century had an air of elegance and sophistication unmatched elsewhere in the world (but unfortunately this facade hid a multitude of social, political and ethnic problems). This period, the so called fin de siècle, is remarkable in that even from this distance in time, it still appears as engaging and spectacular as it did then.

So much has been made of the term "fin de siècle" that it has acquired an almost magical quality for some people, as if the years themselves determined issues, but the term has become a useful reference point for the surge of new movements in philosophy, literature, the visual arts and music in Vienna at the time. The atonal music of Arnold Schoenberg and his disciples held no attraction for Arthur and in the Viennese stories which he told in his later years,

Schoenberg's innovations had no place. Arthur was sustained by the German music of the nineteenth century which still dominated the concert halls. Brahms was living in Vienna until his death in Arthur's middle student years and Mahler, who became his musical hero, was at the helm of the Opera and the Vienna Philharmonic.

The American historian, Carl Schorske, taking music as the dominant Viennese culture, used Maurice Ravel's *La Valse* as a symbol of the times, describing it as a grotesque memorial of the violent death of the nineteenth-century Viennese world in which the gay waltz became increasingly a frantic *danse macabre*. Composed in 1922, the music recalls the political and cultural destruction of Europe and particularly the Austro-Hungarian Empire. Nevertheless, this process began a lot earlier and the turn-of-the-century happened to be the turning point. The balls and the waltzes and operettas were still the symbol of Viennese social life when the young graduate made his choices, but the political and social forces which led to Ravel's composition were already now playing underneath the music of Lehar and the Strauss dynasty, clearly audible to those who would listen.

These forces had been brewing for the previous fifty years, almost since the Emperor had ascended his throne, and it had become obvious to many that the Habsburg Empire was entering its last stage. Nationalism was increasing rapidly among the subject peoples of the Empire, and where groups of them moved into Austria, there were ethnic tensions between them and the old-established Viennese. On all sides there were demands for independence. The Austrians themselves were tiring of Imperial control and their representatives in Parliament became increasingly fractious among themselves.

These destructive political forces also resulted in a premature end to what could have been Arthur Schüller's half-century. Had he but known it, Schüller had only fourteen years in which to do his life's major work, after which the opportunities for further development would be denied him or, at best, severely limited, not always by a hand other than his own.

The fin de siècle years and those leading up to the First World War were also thought by some to be the golden age for Viennese Jewry. The writer Stefan Zweig recognised the time as one of unrestricted Jewish opportunity watched over by the protective eye of the Emperor, who frowned on anti-Semitism. Hilde Spiel, the Jewish Viennese trained philosopher and cultural historian, described the period as Vienna's Golden Autumn with its peak cultural, scientific and medical achievements in that time.

Not everybody agreed with this assessment, and at the other end of the spectrum was Sigmund Freud, the inveterate critic of the Habsburgs. The citizens of Vienna elected the populist reformer but anti-Semitic Karl Lueger as Mayor of Vienna three times before the Emperor would permit him to assume his position. At the turn-of-the-century half of the professors in the university were Jewish, drawn from all over the Empire, and most of the educated middle class Jewish people in Vienna came from the Czech lands of Bohemia and Moravia.

The only first-hand information about his medical student days comes from Schüller himself. First in his estimate was admission to the celebrated Vienna Physicians Orchestra while he was still a student, which was apparently a rare event. For how long he remained with the orchestra after he graduated is unknown. Schüller had a deep love and knowledge of classical music and recounted that on at least one occasion Gustav Mahler led the orchestra. During his life, Mahler was more highly regarded for his skills as a conductor and was the director of the Vienna Opera Company (*Hofoper* 1897 to 1907); clearly this was a coup for the physicians, but also spoke to the quality of their orchestra. The Schüllers apparently were quite friendly with Mahler, who on one occasion, according to his wife, gave Arthur advice on his violin playing.

Schüller graduated just over five years after he entered the university, somewhat longer than might be expected of a stellar student, suggesting he may have taken on extra subjects or perhaps a period of *Wanderjahr*. He was certainly familiar with the student culture at the University of Heidelberg, suggesting he may have spent some time there.

Be that as it may, Arthur took his final examinations in Vienna gaining what has been described as "the perfect mark", graduating *sub auspiciis Imperatoris Francesci Josephi* on 5 November 1899. Given the multitude of examiners whom he had to satisfy, this was a remarkable achievement and it earned for him the Franz Joseph Prize that the Emperor had instituted shortly after his accession to the throne in 1848.

Schüller claimed that in all that time he was only the second candidate to merit the prize, which took the material form of a bar of black amber set with four huge diamonds, presented in person by the Emperor. The historical evidence is a little different; apparently the prize, a ring, was awarded to two candidates in the university every year and was not awarded at all in earlier years of Franz Joseph's reign.

To further complicate matters, the description of articles seized by the Nazis does not include anything resembling the amber bar with diamonds; however, a smaller and less spectacular commemorative item, a ring, was "left behind" when the Schüllers departed Austria. The ring appears to have been awarded for academic distinction.

Given what we now know of his dismal financial situation immediately after the First World War, the amber bar may well have been sold. Nevertheless, the facts are he did spectacularly well as a medical student and received some sort of major award in recognition. Exactly what the prize was will probably never be known for certain but whatever he won, it came with a far greater prize. Schüller was permitted to choose the specialty, clinic and the professor under whom he wished to train and to nominate when he wished to start.

The prize was recognised in contemporary Vienna as carrying great prestige whereas two famous names, Sigmund Freud and Julius Wagner-Jauregg, a generation earlier who did not conceal their ambition, were disappointed in not achieving the prize. The latter was to become Schüller's chief and to some extent a mentor. In the light of what was to come, it is intriguing to recall that the both these men had contemplated emigration to Australia early in their careers.

Perhaps the most important event in Schüller's early student years was something which occurred away from Vienna; Schüller would not have realised its significance for his future but undoubtedly sensed some of the excitement filtering down to the junior ranks. In November 1895 Wilhelm Conrad Röntgen, Professor of Physics in the University of Würzburg and its Rector, made a chance observation in the course of his research which he exploited during a series of brilliant experimental investigations, resulting in the discovery and the naming of x-rays.

This discovery in large part determined the course of Arthur Schüller's career. After graduating from the University of Vienna in November 1899, he commenced his post graduate medical training the following year.

Town square of Brno now known as Náměstí Srobody, Freedom Square. Arthur Schüller's father, an ENT surgeon, practised from number 4 Grosser Platz, which is the building in the middle.

This imposing apartment block, located at Garnisongasse 7 Vienna, is where Schüller and his family lived. He also carried on his private practice and private teaching in their apartment.

A formal photograph of the Stiassni children, late nineteenth century. Grete is centre with her hand on the arm on her sister Anna. Behind Anna is Helene and next to her is Rudolf, the oldest son, with Alfred to his left standing behind the youngest brother Ernst who was close to Grete in age.

Chapter Two

The Vienna Medical School –
the Making of a Polymath

When Arthur Schüller came to Vienna and the university in the second half of 1894, he found himself in what was called at that time the New, or Second, Vienna Medical School, then at the height of its resurgent fame. It was to remain at the centre of his activities for the rest of his time in Vienna.

The University of Vienna, and with it the medical faculty, was formally established by Duke Rudolf IV of Austria on 12 March 1365. However, to understand how the university had come to be one of the world's foremost educational institutions at the time Schüller arrived, and its medical school a centre of international excellence, we need to look to the middle of the eighteenth century, to the reign of Empress Maria Theresa (1740-80), the only woman in the Habsburg lineage to have ruled in her own right. The Scientific Revolution of the eighteenth century provoked the need for a radical remake of medical teaching, and the Empress' reforms gave high priority to the medical school. Equally important was her son and successor, the Emperor Josef II. Both were visionaries with a determination to introduce reform not only in the medical school but throughout the university, and indeed the Empire.

※

By the middle of the eighteenth century, the old medical faculty in Vienna had lost its lustre and the Dutch medical school of Boerhaave and his disciples in Leyden had risen to the forefront of medical endeavour and training in Europe. At a time when the Netherlands was still part of the Habsburg Empire, Maria Theresa selected Boerhaave's most outstanding pupil, Gerard van Swieten, as her personal physician, bringing him to Vienna and charging him with resurrecting the Vienna Medical School. This he did with remarkable success, the end product becoming known to later historians as the First Vienna Medical School.

Van Swieten's influence was not to be limited to the medical school and, in time, he reorganised the university and all its departments and faculties. He closed the old medical school and hospital in the old University District in the central city and rebuilt it in Alsergrund, a suburb immediately to the north of the old city wall, known from around that time as the ninth district. The Empress did not live to open the new hospital; it was opened by her son the Emperor Josef II in 1784. Known as the Allgemeine Krankenhaus or General Hospital, it became so famous the world over that it has often been referred to just by its German name. The design of the building drew its inspiration from the major infirmary in Paris, the Hôtel-Dieu. It was here that the medical school was located.

By the mid-nineteenth century the need for another rejuvenation of the Vienna Medical School had become apparent. In 1849 Karl Rokitansky was appointed as Professor of Anatomical Pathology and it was he who brought forth the Second Vienna Medical School. Rokitansky convinced the government to require that every person who died in the Allgemeine Krankenhaus be submitted to an autopsy as a matter of law, and much of the autopsy material was preserved and catalogued for future research.

When Arthur Schüller graduated, the hospital was a vast structure consisting of a series of inter-connected courts which accommodated four thousand patients and the associated services they required.

It provided an enormous wealth of clinical material for study and teaching.

⸙

The official records have little or nothing to say about the conditions of study for students in those years, but the testimony of an expert and interested witness such as William Osler is informative. Recently appointed Professor of Medicine in McGill University, Montréal, Osler spent several months in Vienna in 1874, at a time when a considerable number of American and Canadian postgraduate students were already making the pilgrimage to the increasingly famous school to take their specialist postgraduate courses.

Osler was impressed by the quality of research and he thought that the great reputation of the Second Medical School as a centre of medical education and research was well-founded. The bibliophile in Osler was excited by the vast general library in the university, reputed to contain four million volumes, but as a teacher of young students he was not impressed. The undergraduates had virtually no access to the book stacks other than a handful of prescribed texts, and they were all crowded into one small reading room.

As a doctor he was dismayed by the disheveled and dirty state of the wards. Nevertheless, the wealth of clinical material pleased the teacher from Montréal, and he was inclined to be understanding of the financial and overcrowding difficulties the university was suffering.

Osler returned in 1908, this time as the Regius Professor of Medicine at the University of Oxford, after having occupied the chairs of medicine in the University of Pennsylvania and then Johns Hopkins University. He found that the Allgemeine Krankenhaus had been completely rebuilt. Again Osler was impressed with the standard and amount of research and, as a teacher and researcher, enthralled by the volume of clinical experience available to the academic staff, but still disappointed by inadequate standards of cleanliness in the wards. Perhaps this does not call for harsh criticism; finance was already a problem and no doubt they were learning that a four-thousand bed hospital cannot be operated appropriately under one administration, as other institutions in other countries would come to realise.

Further, the Medical School was paying a price for its spectacular success. Undergraduate and postgraduate students flocked from all over the world. Any student with suitable qualifications in the Austro-Hungarian Empire and the other German-speaking countries was entitled to apply for admission to the university. The hospital had been open for only a few years before it was seriously overcrowded, as were the lecture theatres, where many had to stand or sit on the floor. Osler observed the consequences with understanding but disapproval.

In spite of the political unrest, it was a good time and a good place to begin training as a clinician and medical research scientist, a combination which had brought the medical school to its high plateau of outstanding achievements in only fifty years from its renewal as the New or Second Vienna Medical School.

The years before the First World War were arguably the medical school's golden age. Schüller's future teacher and superior, Julius Wagner-Jauregg (1857–1940) was working on fever therapy for cerebral syphilis during these years, for which he was awarded the Nobel Prize in Physiology or Medicine in 1927 (after a long time awaiting general acceptance of his method, which was the only effective treatment before penicillin).

Work in the same period earned two more of Wagner-Jauregg's colleagues the prize: Karl Landsteiner (1930) for his discovery of blood groups and Robert Bárány (1914) for his research on the balance mechanism in the inner ear. The faculty produced other additions to the medical canon, allergy (Clemens von Pirque), as well as the radiological contributions of Arthur Schüller and many others.

And Sigmund Freud was ever present. For many years the medical faculty had recruited the best possible applicants not only from the Empire but from all of Europe, and in turn Vienna was exporting some of its talented people to other countries. However for some, in the light of constant political unrest, Vienna and its medical school were beginning to lose a little of their magical attraction.

The spin of these events tended to throw some internationally established scholars out into other orbits; witness the departure in those years of von Pirquet (to Johns Hopkins University) and Bárány (to Uppsala University) among others. It does not seem likely that the University of Vienna welcomed these movements.

There was at least one aspect of university life Schüller was only too happy to describe. On several occasions, he spoke proudly about never having to defend himself in a duel, pointing to his unscarred face and arms. There might have been an element of romance in this because student dueling at that time usually required the wearing of protective clothing including a padded face mask; but perhaps this was not invariable. Dueling on points of honour was commonplace among the military in the German states of the nineteenth century, usually with pistols, but duels spread to the universities in the form of sword fights using sabers, the slightly curved military swords. Later this practice was imported into the Austrian universities. The wearing of a belted sword on the hip was regarded as the sign and privilege of a gentleman; as part of the lifting of restrictions, Jewish people had been granted the right to bear these arms.

For the most part, such encounters grew out of the political, religious and racial antagonisms which existed between the student clubs (*Burschenschaften*). By the time Arthur got to the university, the challenging of Jewish students, mainly by members of the pan-German groups, was on the wane. Undoubtedly this was in part due to disciplinary action by the university authorities, but it is worth noting that the Jewish students played a major part in discouraging their adversaries. They had taken to training in swordsmanship, some becoming dangerous adversaries, perhaps too dangerous to risk challenging. Many others simply declined to accept the challenge on a point of principle and walked away.

Some of this may have grown out of the story told of their Professor of Anatomy in the Vienna Medical School at that time, Emil Zuckerkandl, who was recognised widely as an expert swordsman. A decade before, when Professor of Anatomy at Linz, Zuckerkandl, had silenced the shouting down of the pan-Germans by throwing a handful of his cards at the feet in the front row, challenging all of them to a duel. Silence fell and the cards were not taken up. Arthur Schüller spoke several times to various acquaintances about the intensity of the student dueling in the University of Heidelberg, perhaps indicating some familiarity with that scene.

Among the ordinary citizens of Vienna, as well as within the university, the corroding popular ethnic anti-Semitism in Vienna remained the same, regardless of religious status, and applied equally to observant Jews, those who had left their faith, and Christian converts alike. Academic preferment and advancement was one thing, but the social difficulties remained. Wagner-Jauregg appointed his assistants on merit but was often unhappy in doing so. This led to the perception that he was anti-Semitic. His biographer Magda Whitrow exonerated him of this more serious charge after concluding that it was "because they were likely to give him more trouble than the gentiles since they encountered more difficulties in their careers". Regardless of what Wagner-Jauregg might have thought, he certainly assisted Schüller in his career and earned his esteem in the process.

Wagner-Jauregg's later years revealed a somewhat different picture. He subscribed to ideas of eugenics and in particular racial purity of the Germanic variety with a strongly anti-Semitic nature. In the late 1930s he applied to join the Nazi party but in a great irony was rejected on the basis of his first wife's Jewish heritage.

As a winner of the Franz Joseph Prize, Schüller chose to specialise in neurology and psychiatry under the direction of Richard Krafft-Ebing and Julius Wagner-Jauregg. Schüller's first contributions to the scientific literature in 1900 and 1901 reflect the influence and interests of these two mentors. The first paper described the effect of a soporific agent and the second, maniacal jealousy in females. The combination of neurology and psychiatry was chosen more often in those times than pure neurology or psychiatry alone. This had something to do with the fascination which psychiatry held for the Austrian mind and something to do with wider professional opportunities. Many of the developments in psychiatry in the early twentieth century came out of Vienna, including insulin shock treatment (Manfred Sakel), chemical treatment of psychiatric illness (Wagner-Jauregg), sexual perversion (Krafft-Ebing) and of course psychoanalysis (Freud).

Exploring the reasons for this, the psychoanalyst Bruno Bettelheim believed it was a Viennese fixation with death and sex as a response to the difficult times. The Professor, Richard Krafft-Ebing, held his chair in both psychiatry and neurology. His department, situated in the General Hospital, had over a hundred psychiatric beds and forty neurology beds. The department included a laboratory for animal research in the anatomy and physiology of the nervous system located on the second floor of the Institute of Anatomical Pathology, just across the street from the hospital. Officially the unit was known as the Second Psychiatric Clinic, the First Clinic being situated in an asylum in the suburbs, also known as the Asylum for Lower Austria.

Julius Wagner-Jauregg was the head of the First Clinic when Arthur Schüller began his intern year in 1900. Previously the Professor of Psychiatry in Graz, he had been appointed to the Vienna chair in 1893, and in consequence of his extraordinary talents had risen to be Dean of the Medical Faculty by 1895. Wagner-Jauregg was fully aware of the young man Schüller and it seems probable that he was responsible for mapping some of his academic program.

In support of Schüller's advancement to the level of professor in 1914, Wagner-Jauregg summarised his career to that stage in a document that is still in existence in the University of Vienna archives. He indicated that Schüller had graduated on 5 November 1899 and commenced his training as "Aspirant" (candidate) on 11 July, but he may have those initial dates confused.

Schüller's other mentor, Krafft-Ebing, head of the Second Psychiatric Clinic, was an ill man at the time Schüller started his studies; he retired in 1902 and died shortly after. Wagner-Jauregg moved to the General Hospital to head up the Second Psychiatric Clinic, giving him the facilities for his particular interest in organic psychiatry and animal research at the Institute of Neurology.

The Institute was a separate organisation founded in 1882 by Heinrich Obersteiner and was the first institution anywhere dedicated solely to neurology research and teaching. Wagner-Jauregg's ambition was to develop successful therapies for illness rather than stopping short at semiology for fear of breaking the commitment to "first do no harm".

Arthur Schüller remained in the Second Clinic after finishing his training, making it the center of his clinical practice for the remainder of his time in Vienna. The Second Clinic eventually merged with and absorbed the First Clinic within the General Hospital under Wagner-Jauregg's leadership several years later. Subsequently his deputy, Otto Pötzl, succeeded him in 1928, and both Wagner-Jauregg and Pötzl promoted Schüller's cause for the remainder of his career. There was no clinic in the hospital specifically for clinical neurology at the turn of the century and the majority of the neurology patients were admitted to the First Department of Medicine headed by Hermann Nothnagel. He was widely regarded in the German-speaking countries as the last man to know all there was to know in medicine. He was also an active opponent of anti-Semitism.

After completing his intern year, Schüller spent six months in a study program at the University of Berlin under Hermann Munk, the professor of physiology. This arrangement was no doubt organised by his mentors and, at first sight, it appeared to indicate that he was destined exclusively for a career in experimental physiology and anatomy of the nervous system, but other remarkable opportunities came with it.

Munk was in active collaboration with Hermann Oppenheim, the foremost clinical neurologist in Germany, arguably in Continental Europe. Oppenheim had been the deputy director of the Neurology

Clinic at the Charité Hospital in the Medical School of the University in Berlin until 1890, when he was expected to succeed the retiring director. He had been chosen unanimously by the university authorities, but the Prussian Secretary for Education intervened to block the appointment. The reasons for this are obscure, but petty jealousy and his membership of the Central Association for Citizens of the Jewish Faith appear to be the most likely. Ultimately he was forced to leave the clinic and the Charité, to which he responded by establishing a highly successful private clinic and research institute in the Augusta Hospital in Berlin.

Postgraduate students in neurology came from all over Germany and beyond. Arthur's study program included attendance at all ward rounds, lectures and other teaching sessions in Oppenheim's Institute as well as his activities in Munk's laboratory.

Working in the same institute was Fedor Krause, the Professor of Surgery in the University of Berlin, and the leading surgeon in Germany. He had a strong interest in developing neurosurgery, in which regard he was ahead of his Viennese colleagues. At that time Oppenheim was working on the clinical diagnosis of brain tumours and exploring the possibilities of surgical treatment in collaboration with Krause, to whom he referred his patients. Both men were active in the literature, contributing articles on brain tumours and their treatment in the journals.

Oppenheim published a book on the diagnosis and treatment of his cases in 1896 and another in 1907; Krause summarised his experience in the operative surgery of brain tumours and the relief of trigeminal neuralgia in 1906. All of this work would have been part of the daily round during Arthur's time in Berlin; what twenty-five-year-old could have resisted the excitement of this stimulus? Further, Oppenheim had published the first recorded case of diagnosis of a pituitary tumour by x-ray, which in this instance revealed an abnormally expanded sella turcica in a woman with acromegaly and progressive blindness. This might have been Arthur Schüller's first experience of a slowly growing mass thinning and deforming of the adjacent bone structure of the skull.

⚜

In Munk's laboratory, Schüller was encouraged to investigate the function of the caudate nucleus. For the last half of the nineteenth century, the caudate nucleus and other structures had attracted much interest, but the work of previous researchers, using small laboratory animals, had produced inconclusive results. This is not surprising because the surgical approach meant a craniotomy followed by the removal of the hemisphere overlying the target and the need to then approach it through the ventricle. The result was massive damage to systems other than the caudate nucleus.

Others, going back to early in the nineteenth century, had attempted blind needle insertion, which hints at stereotactic thinking even then. These observations led the budding scientist Schüller to seek alternatives which might permit destruction of the nucleus with minimal damage to surrounding tissues and structures.

He began by reviewing the gross anatomy of the dog's brain with coronal sections after fixing. He noted that the head of the nucleus and the tail almost sat in the same sagittal plane with a slight lateral curvature which, if extended anteriorly, would emerge through the frontal sinus a short distance from the midline of the skull. Provided that the angle of insertion of an instrument was accurate, it could be inserted through a very small skin incision followed by small holes in the anterior and posterior walls of the frontal sinus, made with a small chisel, followed by a small incision in the dura and frontal cortex.

Here he was relying on his remarkable ability to visualise deep brain structures but it was still necessary to construct an instrument for making the lesion. Schüller began with a straight metal rod to the circumference of which short lengths of spring wire were attached in a radial configuration, resembling a bottlebrush. He then slid a metal tube over this assembly so that when pushed along the rod it flattened the wire bristles against the side of the rod. The instrument was inserted with the wire end first until the tip was considered to be in the target region. The outer tube was then withdrawn a short distance to uncover the wire brush, which was rotated to destroy the tissues. But he went further; the rod could be extended along the line of the tail of the nucleus to make further lesions there. This was followed by restoring the outer cover to its original position to push the wire bristles flat against the stem before removing the instrument.

Then, noting that the tail of the nucleus curved slightly laterally, he refined the method. He produced an instrument along the same lines but which had bristles only on one side of its circumference. A lesion could be inflicted on the tail if the rod was only lying beside it, by pointing the bristles in the correct direction.

This was a sophisticated method for the time; readers might be forgiven for believing that they were reading here the latest contribution in the neurosurgical journals of the 1960s. Tissue enmeshed in the bristles was washed off and subjected to histologic staining. The final confirmation came later when the dog was euthanised, the brain removed and fixed and subjected to serial sectioning.

This was a remarkable piece of work which signaled the development of human stereotactic surgery forty years before its time. Arthur Schüller had defined the necessary principles of stereotactic surgery on the brain: a small incision in the scalp and skull, an appropriate angle of approach, a precise knowledge of the relevant anatomy illustrated with meticulous accuracy in a photographic atlas of the morphology and position of the deep brain structures, and an instrument which did little damage in its passage but had the capacity to make lesions in the region of interest and of the desired size. He fell short on one point only, x-ray control, but he had not yet begun his work on cranial radiology.

Shortly after, Victor Horsley and Robert Clark, working in the Department of Physiology at University College London, independently conceived the idea of a rigid frame which would immobilise the head of small experimental animals to allow the use of highly accurate aiming devices mounted on the frame. Work on the Horsley-Clarke stereotactic apparatus began in 1905 but it took three years to develop the system to its final state.

Their paper was published in 1908 and it contains no reference to Schüller's work, which was published in 1902, and almost certainly not known to them at the time.

Many years later, in 1949, Arthur Schüller was working at, St Vincent's Hospital in Melbourne at the time when Frank Morgan, the neurosurgeon, was proposing to perform a recently published surgical procedure for Parkinson's disease. The operation involved exposure of the frontal lobe by a standard craniotomy, followed by an incision through the cortex and sub-cortical white-matter to enter the frontal horn of the lateral ventricle. This allowed an approach to the caudate nucleus and internal capsule across the cavity of the ventricle.

This procedure aroused Schüller's memories of his work with dogs at the beginning of the century and he urged Morgan to use a stereo-tactic approach, using an atlas of normal-sized brain sections to derive the depth of penetration and its trajectory from a frontal burr-hole.

A simple strip of flexible steel sheet mounted with a short length of brass tubing to guide the probe was made up in the hospital work-shop to the professor's design, but Morgan was not moved. Schüller was very disappointed by Morgan's rejection but it was clearly the appropriate decision.

Ironically, the first successful stereotactic operations on human subjects had been reported in 1947 by Ernest Spiegel and Henry Wycis working at Temple University in Philadelphia. The science for the procedure came from Spiegel, previously a colleague of Arthur Schüller in the Institute of Neurology in Vienna. Both men had subsequently left their homeland, Spiegel in 1931 and Schüller in 1938, following the German annexation of Austria. At the time of the operation, Spiegel's work was unknown to both Morgan and Schüller.

In his six months in Berlin, Schüller the Aspirant had been exposed to experimental physiology, clinical neurology, the diagnosis and treat-ment of brain tumours and the radiological phenomenon of bone changes indicating the presence of an adjacent expanding mass.

We do not know who was responsible for driving Schüller's investigation of the potential of radiology in the diagnosis of diseases of the nervous system, but it seems inescapable that Wagner-Jauregg was the major influence.

Schüller returned to Vienna in 1901 to a storm of activity, both clinical and experimental. He resumed his training as a psychiatrist and neurologist in the Second Psychiatric Clinic. He finished his training position on 1 March 1904, but some time prior to this he was appointed as assistant in the Second Psychiatric Clinic, to which he maintained a link till he left Austria nearly forty years later.

At the same time, his clinical career was also boosted by his appointment in October 1900 as an assistant physician to Professor Emil Redlich in the neurology clinic at the Children's Hospital, within walking distance from his home. Schüller rose rapidly in the ranks to become Vorstand or Director of the unit in 1904, succeeding Redlich who retired two years later. It seems that his mentors were set on a career for him in pediatric neurology, along with basic neuroscience as the next priority.

Munk had encouraged him to publish his work on the caudate nucleus once his experiments were completed back in Vienna. This he did almost immediately under the tutelage of Professor Richard Paltauf, the Director of the Institute of Experimental Pathology. This paper was published in 1902, reporting only a slight advance in knowledge. The procedure was done under anesthesia from which the experimental animal, a dog, would recover and survive for at least a few days in a state which permitted clinical examination to determine the effects of the procedure. There was an inconsistent tendency for the dogs to turn towards the side of the surgical lesion, leading Schüller to speculate that the caudate had some function as a "turning centre". He had at least revealed a motor function, however insignificant.

It was in the laboratory where he conducted this research that Wagner-Jauregg also did his own experimental work, and it is reasonable to conclude that he also had a hand in the training of the neophyte physiologist during this period.

In 1906 Arthur was presented with another experimental task. Some years previously Wagner-Jauregg and one of his assistants had explored the effect of bilateral section of the pyramidal tract on motor function. They failed to demonstrate that the tract had a specific motor function. But Arthur Schüller was to make another attempt. Much of the previous work on deep brain structures had necessarily been crude, often involving wide craniotomy and damage to the overlying hemisphere in the process of reaching the target nucleus. It was clear that a new experimental design was necessary.

Schüller began with a detailed analysis of the previous work done in the second half of the nineteenth century, which led him to believe that the situation of the pyramid on the ventral surface of the medulla oblongata required a direct approach through the base of the skull rather than the destructive, bilateral (both sides) pyramidal section procedure previously advocated by Wagner-Jauregg. Schüller's solution was to divide one pyramid only, placing the incision considerably higher above the decussation of the pyramidal fibres which resulted in far less tissue damage to neighbouring tracts and nuclear groups. Furthermore he confined the procedure to one side only, allowing the results to be compared with the normal situation on the other side.

Fortuitously, one of Schüller's earliest research projects in neurology was a detailed clinical analysis of patients with hemiplegia which had resulted from a variety of causes. Determination of the cause relied on clinical history and examination for many patients but, for others, detailed autopsy studies were available (1903). For those who could walk, he confirmed the old observation that the paralysed limb with partial recovery was used in a circumductory movement. In other words, the legs could move forwards and backwards and stand with support, and some abduction was possible, but adduction of the affected limb was impossible. From an analysis of these cases he confirmed the findings in experimental animals that the failure of adduction was the result of interruption of the pyramidal tract, even though many previous studies had clearly demonstrated that many other motor pathways were also involved in the causal disease process.

He concluded that the failure of adduction was pathognomonic of damage to the pyramidal tract. Turning to this, he investigated the ability of the patient to step sideways, a manoeuvre which he called "flank walking". Failure of flank walking was to be the essential indicator in the animal study that the experimental lesion had successfully sectioned the pyramid.

The surgery was performed under general anesthesia, and both dogs and monkeys were used. The endotracheal tube for anesthesia had yet to be invented so the procedure required preliminary tracheostomy. The trachea and related neck structures were displaced to one side and bone drilled out of the anterior arch of the atlas and the anterior rim of the foramen magnum to reveal the dura. This was incised longitudinally to display the anterior surface of the lower brain stem, the pyramids and the decussation of the pyramidal tracts. The lesion in the pyramid was made immediately above the decussation using a very fine angled knife from among the ophthalmological instruments. The vertebral arteries and the lower basilar were also displayed and carefully avoided; it appears that there was no attempt to seal the dural incision.

The animals were then subjected to frequent and repeated clinical examinations beginning within an hour or two of the operation and repeated each day for four weeks in which time the clinical picture was found to be stable after a period of early improvement.

In the first paragraphs of his report, he provides a long, in places tortuous and detailed analysis of the basis for his findings which include an element of defence against the expected challenges from his colleagues:

> If we have been able to show that after one sided isolated pyramid
> injury certain movement disturbances occur at the opposite

extremities, disturbances which fulfil the requirements of an individual movement and which remain almost completely the same over the course of the three-weeks-long observation period, then surely we have the right to consider the pyramidal pathways as the only intermediary for the impulse that allows the completion of this movement.

He summarised the article as follows:

The results of this operation appear as the elimination of certain movement in the individual movements, the most apparent being the adduction and abduction of limbs when walking sideways. These disturbances appear immediately after the operation and are not complicated by the appearance of other function disturbances which appear, for example in cortical extirpation, and persist unchanged throughout the observation period. Because of this we do not believe that we have simply found one symptom of pyramidal lesion but rather that we have proven one of the exclusive functions of the pyramidal pathways.

Schüller must have been content with the outcome of his research; he did not take it any further thereafter and his conclusions were not challenged in the medical press. Nevertheless, it is clear from his publications that he retained an interest in laboratory work and continued to work on various experimental surgical techniques.

Other aspects of Schüller's clinical work provided opportunities for his laboratory work. In the Clinic for Psychiatry and Neurology he encountered patients who had syphilis of the nervous system involving the dorsal roots and spinal cord, resulting in paroxysmal spasms or severe pain, the so-called "lightning pains" in the limbs and trunk (1906). There was no satisfactory treatment for these and it seems that he became attracted to the idea of some form of surgical remedy.

At the Children's Hospital he certainly came into contact with children suffering from, among other problems, cerebral palsy and spastic paralysis. For some years the idea of sectioning the dorsal roots of spinal nerves for these and other conditions had come under increasing scrutiny, supported by the explosion in knowledge in the second half of the nineteenth century of the micro-anatomy and physiology of the spinal cord. Here the lightning pains of neuro-syphilis and spasticity of children came together, sharing the possible benefits of section of the nerve roots.

Arthur Schüller did not conceive these operative procedures, but he now set about replicating them and assessing them in the laboratory, practising on experimental animals. His persistence with animal experimental surgery and the accumulation of the results of surgery on human subjects would have revealed to him that there was something beneficial to the use of dorsal root section for both these groups of patients, in spite of a significant failure rate and a significant mortality.

The first refinements of the necessary indications for dorsal root section came from Otfrid Foerster of Breslau, who established its use for the treatment of young people with cerebral palsy and severe spas-ticity. The relief of spasticity necessitated division of the sensory roots of the spinal nerves immediately before they entered the spinal cord with preservation of the motor nerve roots by careful and accurate assessment of the nerve roots.

In most cases, it was necessary to divide multiple roots, which demanded an extensive laminectomy to achieve long exposure of the spinal cord. This was major surgery which was often too much both for children and sick syphilitic adults, and unfortunately had quite variable results.

Arthur Schüller was not a surgeon and therefore he played no part in this surgical management, but he was familiar with it from the work of other surgeons in the hospital and in other hospitals in the Vienna region. He had neurologically assessed some of their patients before and after the operations. As usual, he was soon ready to submit advice to his surgical colleagues, which doubtless was well received, at the weekly meetings and later in the form of publications in the local journals.

It appears that he began a series of experimental operations on animals in the hope of finding a way to improve the results of surgery for human subjects, and to limit the long and burdensome operations for them. His principal concern was the alleviation of the dreadful lightning pains in the lower limbs and trunk in the neurosyphilis cases. He was aware that all painful impulses reached consciousness by way of the spinothalamic tract, which was reasonably safe to access surgically. (Previous procedures for controlling spasticity or lightning pains had involved division of sensory nerve roots after their exit from the spinal cord. His approach, based on his deep understanding of the relevant anatomy and physiology was to directly incise the sensory fibres of the spinothalamic tract within the spinal cord i.e. cordotomy.)

In reports of his research on cordotomy, Schüller presented an analysis of the risks and difficulties which he had worked out in a series of operations on animals, mainly dogs and monkeys. His analysis demonstrated that surgical section of the tract was readily achieved without significant damage to the adjacent motor pathways. He acknowledged that the central nervous system, i.e. the brain and spinal cord – as opposed to the peripheral structures such as cranial nerves and spinal nerves – had thus far been *nolli me tangere* (do not touch me), except for the collateral damage unavoidable in tumour surgery.

He presented his credentials at the Vienna Society of Physicians meeting by demonstrating that section of the spinothalamic tract abolished all painful sensation below the level of the operation by outlining the analgesic areas on the skin of the animals. Furthermore, the animals showed no evidence of motor paralysis, as testimony to his precise and careful technique and knowledge of neuroanatomy. Apparently his colleagues did not hurry to embrace his recommendations for the treatment of lightning pains but at least part of the idea was picked up two years later by William Spiller and Edward Martin when they read Schüller's journal article in the original German. Working in Philadelphia, Martin, spurred on by the physician Spiller, performed the first "anterolateral cordotomy", as it came to be called, for people with secondary cancer, an indication which was quickly adopted and used widely.

꧁꧂

It is not surprising that the Vienna surgeons did not rush to use this procedure; the Vienna medical school had a fifty-year tradition of avoiding new treatments until they were certain that they would "first do no harm". But even there, cordotomy soon had its day. Arthur Schüller had presented his method as a treatment for lightning pains due to syphilis which presented a major problem for patients and those people who cared for them.

On the other hand, Spiller and Martin were dealing with cancer every day in some part of the body, and they therefore had this as their point of departure. In their paper they acknowledged his publication, but dismissed it because he had not developed the operation for cancer, which was the major indication in the vast majority of patients worldwide. The fact that Schüller had worked out the details of the procedure which Spiller and Martin applied for a different diagnosis was perhaps a little egregious. This was a great disappointment for Schüller, who put great store on his achievements, but he did not complain.

Regardless of any lack of recognition, Schüller's work laid the way for significant advances in surgery. Until this time surgeons had avoided damaging any pathways or nuclei within the central nervous system itself, except in the case of brain tumours. Schüller had demonstrated through his careful research on laboratory animals that such an operation could achieve its desired purpose without discoverable damage to other nerve fibre systems. His research thus opened the door to human cordotomy and, more significantly, to stereotactic surgery for the relief of Parkinson's disease and other movement disorders when it was introduced thirty years later by his Viennese colleague Ernest Spiegel in Philadelphia, the same city where Spiller and Martin reported the first cordotomy.

꧁꧂

After Schüller's formal training in neurology and psychiatry finished in the early years of the twentieth century, the remaining ten years until the start of the First World War were an extraordinary period of professional achievement and personal development. What has been recounted in this chapter was the laboratory-based experimental neurological research. Many of his ideas presaged subsequent developments in neurosurgery, including cisternal puncture, drainage of hydrocephalus, cordotomy for intractable pain and stereotactic approaches to the brain. It is extraordinary to remember that, in addition to this large body of innovative and groundbreaking research, he made his career as a neurologist, and at the same time set the foundations for what was to become modern neuroradiology. To think that his clinical, radiological and laboratory research were separate endeavours would be unreasonable. They relied on a deep understanding of anatomy and its relation to normal function or physiology and an understanding of diseases of the central nervous system, in particular the pathological processes and increasingly their radiological hallmarks.

It has been claimed that Schüller had done most of his great work before 1914, with the inevitable conclusion that there was not much to follow. There is some truth to this observation, as most of the work he is remembered for occurred early in his career. Review of his published works indicates that in the years leading up to the First World War he was remarkably productive, with the two textbooks and numerous articles which made his fame.

By 1915, his academic output had slowed and only three papers were published that year, none in 1916 and two in 1917. A further two papers were published in 1918 and there was only a small increase in his output until the mid to late 1920s when his academic output increased again, quantitatively if not qualitatively. The timing of this major hiatus in his academic output would suggest that the First World War and its devastating effects must have had a profound effect on his career. The reduction in his academic output by 1915 would certainly support this notion. There are no records extant of a personal nature from this period, but later Schüller did muse that the First World War and its aftermath were a personal and financial disaster for him.

Schüller's extraordinary academic performance in the period running up to the war was matched with developments in his personal life. In December 1906 he married Margarete (Grete) Stiassni.[1] She was twelve years his junior and it appears to have been something of an arranged marriage. Her family were well established and successful in the textile trade in Brno.

Their first meeting was in the Sacher Hotel, a favourite meeting place for concertgoers after an evening at the Vienna Opera or the Philharmonic. Her parents maintained a box there during the season.

The newlyweds moved to a rented apartment at 7 Garnisongasse, within walking distance of both the university and the hospital where they were to remain till they left Vienna for Australia. Not only was this where the Schüllers and their two sons Franz (born 1908) and Hans (born 1909) lived, but where he gave private tutorials (in the European fashion the attendees paid the professor) and ran a private practice including an early x-ray machine he installed in 1905.

It has been widely supposed that Arthur Schüller chose to convert to Christianity at about the beginning of his academic career. There is some support for this notion from members of Arthur's wife, Grete Stiassni's family. Though registered in the university both as a student and a faculty member as a Jew, Schüller was certainly a baptised Catholic by the early years of the century. Some present-day members of his future wife's family believe that Christianity entered the family with Arthur's father; however, both of Arthur's parents were buried in the Jewish cemetery in Brno, where they lived.

Professor Erwin Schindler, Professor of Neuroradiology in the University of Vienna, had researched this point as far as it could be taken and he concluded that the Stiassni family were probably right.

A record of Resignation from the Jewish Faith dated 1908 exists for both Arthur and Marguerite shortly after they married in 1906 but no record of a civil or Catholic marriage can be found.

In 2019, search of a recently available online database confirmed that Arthur and Grete were baptised on 15 May 1908 in Vienna at the church of St Peter. Possibly they married outside of Vienna in Brno where Grete's family had also come from. There is support from Stiassni family recollection that they were married in a Catholic church (Susan Martin, Grete's niece). If they were married in 1906 and only renounced their Jewish faith in 1908, the year they were both baptised, it is highly unlikely they would have been married in the Catholic faith.

Why they renounced Judaism is unknown, but given that the Schüllers were already married (the previous year) and he had made steady academic progression by that time, it was probably more of a personal than pragmatic decision. There is no information on whether their two sons were baptised.

Nothing is known of the religious affiliations of the other members of Grete's family, the Stiassnis, but whatever, the consequences were eventually tragic. Her family believe that she was baptised prior to her wedding to Arthur but as noted above this appears to be incorrect and most likely represents the effects of time on family remembrances.

It was further supposed by many that the Schüllers conversion to Christianity was prompted by the widespread view at the time that it would help to promote his university career. This may have been the case and we have no evidence either way. It seems a little surprising, considering that half of the professors in the University of Vienna in the year 1900 were in fact from Jewish families, and only a tiny minority of them had been baptised and even fewer were practising Christians. A similar proportion of the academic staff were "dismissed" from the university (over 1600) in 1938, mainly as a consequence of their Jewish heritage. Thus it appears that Christianity may not have been such a significant influence in academic advancement or indeed appointment in the first place.

Nothing is known of his wife's relationship with Catholicism but in Australia she was remembered as steadfast a Catholic as her husband. On the papers Schüller filled out on arrival in Australia in 1939, he described his race as Jewish.

In 1907 Schüller was awarded the advanced qualification of *Habilitiert fur Neurologie und Psychiatrie* (or formal recognition of research excellence and would be equivalent to a doctoral examination) and granted the *Venia Docendi*, the formal authorisation to teach within the university. The qualification process included a formal evaluation of his academic output by the university and suitable testimonials from his superiors.

The recommendation from his old chief Wagner-Jauregg is an impressive listing of his accomplishments justifying his promotion (University of Vienna Archives). It was an important milestone for young academics in the University of Vienna on track towards professorship. When Schüller was granted professorship in January 1914, at the age of forty, he was the youngest professor in the Medical School.

In addition to his appointment in the Second Psychiatric Clinic at the General Hospital, Schüller held appointments in neurology at the Children's Hospital and at the Franz Joseph Ambulatorium. The latter was a predominantly outpatient-based clinic dedicated to research and education. He was associated with the Institute of Neurology, the research department of the Second Psychiatric Clinic, and had an informal relationship with Holznecht and his successors in the nascent Department of Radiology of the Second Medical Clinic (eventually the Central Röntgen Laboratory) in the General Hospital.

In a university roster of staff from 1932, Schüller is listed as belonging to not only the Second Psychiatric Clinic but also the radiology department (Central Roentgen Laboratory). He maintained an association with the University of Vienna, enjoying the rank and privileges as one of its most productive members.

His university position gave him the right to receive payment for teaching, and by 1914 his reputation as a neurologist and an expert in the developing field of radiology of the central nervous system meant he was not without a heavy teaching load. His opinion on difficult cases was frequently sought, and increasingly foreign visitors came to observe and learn.

⁂

The outbreak of the First World War brought disaster to Austria and to Schüller. The Army was not well equipped, there was friction with the German High Command and the Austrians fared badly on their eastern and southern fronts. Casualties were heavy and army medical services overwhelmed.

Little is known of Schüller's experience of the First World War but it is clear he did not serve in a theatre of war. There has been a suggestion that he avoided direct military service on health grounds, possibly due to issues with his feet, presumably the early stages of the radiation dermatitis that was to affect him for the rest of his life.

Schüller was involved, however, in the war effort in the care of injured servicemen, and according to his Australian entry documents had been a member of the Austrian army. During the war, Vienna played a critical role as a military logistics centre and a major producer of war materials. For most of the war, the city was under direct military control.

In 1910, Vienna had a population of 2.1 million people and during the war the numbers increased by approximately 15 per cent, despite the absence of large numbers of able-bodied men away at the front. A flood of refugees descended upon the city, many from the Austro-Hungarian Emperor's lands that were lost during the fighting, particularly in the east. There was a desperate need for medical services, as Vienna's position as a military and transport hub ensured that large numbers of casualties were received in the city. In 1915, 260,000 casualties arrived in Vienna.

By 1916, seven new hospitals had been built and a large number of other buildings were converted to hospitals and recuperation centres. The need for medical services, already at breaking point due to the influx of the wounded and refugees, was worsened by other health issues related to poor hygiene, food shortages and overcrowding, with a significant increase in the incidence of tuberculosis and cholera throughout the city.

As the war years went on, the incidence of "shell-shock" rose steeply. The case numbers overwhelmed the system, and new dedicated hospitals for the care of these patients were opened in the Vienna suburbs. The symptoms were essentially neurologic conversions, ataxia, tremors, spasms and paralyses as well as fits, faints and dizziness.

The distinction between neurosis and malingering was problematical and treatment was controversial and difficult, and called for neurological and psychiatric expertise. This is how Schüller spent his war under the direction of the military. His work in the animal experimental laboratory stopped and appears never to have been resumed; perhaps the time was given over to postgraduate lecturing in skull radiology.

In 1918 and 1919 he published two substantial articles on war neuroses; among other matters, they contained a critique of Freud's theories and methods, cautiously concluding that they might be effective in other "hysterical" states. He did not, at that time, see psychoanalysis becoming a lifestyle statement.

As for most other Viennese, life changed immeasurably for the Schüllers during the war. Food rationing was severe and was maintained at the insistence of the French until 1920. Conditions became so bad that the eventually the Americans were forced to intervene. The rampant inflation depleted the savings of many, and with the failure of the banks towards the end of the war, life was difficult, even for the relatively well off like the Schüllers.

Immediately after the war the university asked Wagner-Jauregg to organise a greatly expanded program of postgraduate courses across the whole medical spectrum and advertise to the world. The world duly came, particularly from America. The Vienna Medical School had been the most celebrated medical centre in the world since the advent of Karl von Rokitansky as the Professor of Pathological

Anatomy in the middle of the nineteenth century.

Schüller was heavily involved in this postgraduate program in addition to his other duties, developing a course entitled "Radiology from the standpoint of the neurologist". His unrivaled knowledge, his teaching skills, his command of English and, one suspects, his personality assured its success. From among the many who attended, he made numerous friends from many countries. The American neurosurgeon Walter Edward Dandy, who first described ventriculography and encephalography, visited Schüller in Vienna in 1924 and was to become a close friend, being a noteworthy example.

In reality, Schüller's professional world fell apart during the war years and immediately after. The war was unpopular, indeed bitterly resisted, and early in 1916 the Prime Minister was assassinated in a restaurant by the pacifist son of Victor Adler, the founder of the Social Democrats Party of which Schüller is believed to have been a member. The Emperor died a few months later. He had been in large measure the cause of the increasing demands of his many subject peoples for national independence but, paradoxically, loyalty to his person, a way of life for his peoples for sixty years, endured and remained the only possible remedy against disintegration. With his death, that reason was gone and the game was up.

His youthful successor, his nephew Karl I, could not resist the internal drive for dismemberment and redistribution of the empire. In any case the Allies, headed by Woodrow Wilson, were already planning to do this for him and he was forced into abdication in 1918 and exile in 1919. And so began The First Austrian Republic, which rapidly descended into political anarchy, financial chaos and widespread poverty.

Astronomical inflation and the failure of his bank destroyed Schüller's personal wealth, from which he claimed he never fully recovered, and to add further insult, the impoverished university reduced academic salaries. He conducted a private practice in neurology in his home at night, complete with his own x-ray unit, and to this he added private radiology lessons to postgraduates to make ends meet. Students later fondly remembered the professor leaning on the piano in the living room of his apartment, animatedly lecturing with the assistance of the x-ray light box also perched on the piano.

This practice of private tutorials, although routine in Vienna and elsewhere in Europe in those times, was to get him into trouble later in Australia. The difficult times notwithstanding, the medical school continued to make brilliant contributions and his stream of papers was maintained. Medical visitors after the war were amazed that such a proud and influential university and even the General Hospital could function, given the impoverished and rundown facilities. Even x-ray film was scarce.

Comment has been made that Schüller had done all his great work by 1914 and that in the years after the war, he was a distracted man who spread himself too thinly. With regard to his academic career, these comments are harsh and at least partly correct, but in light of the historical context and the personal and financial difficulties he encountered, his behaviour was understandable.

His laboratory work ceased at the start of the war and was never restarted. In reality, Schüller had no opportunity to turn his consider-able intellect to the next phase in the development of neuroradiology, specifically the imaging of non-bone structures within the skull which came to define modern neuroradiology.

Governments of both the right and left did a remarkable job in salvaging Austria from the wreckage after the war, but the nineteen years of the first republic were rarely tranquil for long. They were punctuated by two workers' uprisings which almost amounted to brief civil wars, one of which ended with an artillery bombardment of tenements in the workers' district in Vienna. The murder of the Austrian Chancellor in a failed coup by a group from the Austrian Nazi Party in 1934 was preceded by a series of bombings of public utilities and institutions, all covertly directed by Hitler.

While all this was going on, Schüller had a local distraction in the shape of student anti-Semitism. Always just below the surface or quietly simmering, it was exacerbated from time to time by activists, chief among whom were the youth groups of the Austrian Nazi Party who brought the violence to new heights. There were riots, brawls and bashings of Jewish students, and Jewish professors had their lectures disrupted by uproar and shouts of "*Juden raus!*". By 1933 the Jewish professor of anatomy, Julius Tandler, could lecture in peace only to Jewish students, while other staff members, presumably including Eduard Pernkopf of anatomical atlas fame, and a Nazi sympathiser, taught the rest.

Vienna transport identification card, second half 1926.

Schüller's personal bookplate.

Formal photograph (date unknown),
probably in 1920s.

Formal portrait of Arthur Schüller
taken around 1930.

Chapter Three

Image and Imagination: Neuroradiology

Solitary meditative observation is the first step in the poetry of research, in the formation of scientific fantasies the reality of which we then test with the tools of logic, mathematics, physics and chemistry.

— Theodor Billroth

On 28 December 1895, nearly eighteen months after Schüller entered the University of Vienna, and on exactly his twenty-first birthday, Wilhelm Conrad Röntgen, Professor of Physics in the University of Würzburg, announced his discovery of x-rays to the world. He chose the Physical-Medical Society in Würzburg for his announcement, where it was the usual practice to present the work in the form of a lecture at a regular meeting of the society and then to publish it in the relevant journal.

In this case, though, the editor decided that immediate publication was necessary and the order was reversed. Röntgen submitted the manuscript on 28 December and had the printed copies available on New Year's Day 1895, which he mailed out to selected scientific colleagues on the same day.

One preprint and copies of the first radiographs went to Franz Exner, the Professor of Physics in Vienna, a previous student of Röntgen's, and he immediately called his brother Sigmund, the

Professor of Physiology, and several other senior doctors from the medical school to his home. Within a few days a crude x-ray apparatus had been assembled from available laboratory equipment.

As early as 10 January, Sigmund Exner presented Röntgen's work to the Society of Physicians of Vienna. It appears that the friendship between Röntgen and Franz Exner started the discussions of possible applications of Röntgen's discovery to medicine. Sigmund, the physiologist, invited his colleague Professor Edmund Neusser, the director of the Second Medical Clinic, to direct patients to his brother Franz Exner in the Physics Department in the University of Vienna.

Gustav Kaiser, Neusser's assistant, was tasked with undertaking these early x-ray studies which were performed in the old Department of Physics building on Turkenstrasse.

Röntgen presented his own work for the first time to the Physical Medical Society in Wurzburg on 23 January 1896, but remarkably, one week earlier on 17 January Sigmund Exner had given a presentation to the Society of Physicians of Vienna demonstrating the first radiographs. The three radiographs that he presented demonstrated the extraordinary benefits of this new technology: the first x-ray was of the hand of a student forest ranger who had undergone an unsuccessful surgical exploration for a retained shot gun pellet; the second was of a young girl with an extra toe, demonstrating that it did not articulate with the terminal phalanx, and the third demonstrated a poorly-healed fracture of a child's forearm. All three patients were successfully operated on.

Gustav Kaiser continued running an x-ray service from a small laboratory in the Second Medical Clinic, and this became the basis for the famous Central Röntgen Laboratory. Guido Holzknecht took over direction of the Institute in 1902, when Kaiser was forced to step down as a consequence of severe radiation injuries sustained in the course of his work. By 1914 the Central Röntgen Laboratory was an independent entity and Kaiser, together with his colleague Robert Kienböck, brought about the Viennese Radiological School.

Late in 1901 or early in 1902 Arthur Schüller approached Wagner-Jauregg, or perhaps the approach came from the opposite direction, with the idea of exploring the potential of x-rays in the diagnosis of diseases of the brain. On their own, x-rays are unable to directly demonstrate any brain structure not impregnated with calcium salts, so Schüller and Wagner-Jauregg's idea must have seemed at first sight to be a forlorn example of an imagination which was not based on the facts as they were known at that time. The x-ray photograph of the calvarium had little to show, other than diseases and deformities of the bones themselves; for the most part it presented a blank screen onto which no brain image was projected. Nevertheless Wagner-Jauregg, who had pushed the development of radiology in the medical school with enthusiasm, sent Schüller off to see Guido Holzknecht in the Central Röntgen Laboratory at the General Hospital.

Frank Morgan, who became Arthur Schüller's great friend in his Australian years, recounted an amusing version of how Arthur came to work with Guido Holzknecht. Arthur said that he was walking in the grounds of the hospital one day when he met Holzknecht, who said "Come, little Schüller, come and join me in the Röntgen Department." There was a tinge of friendly humour here because Guido Holzknecht was only two years older than Schüller, had been only one year ahead in his training, and he had not won a Franz Joseph Prize as had Schüller.

Be the story as it may, Holzknecht had an impressive career in front of him which had already been recognised by his seniors. He graduated a year before Schüller and had gone straight to the Second Medical Clinic under Professor Herbert Nothnagel, where he was immediately put to work on the clinic's own x-ray equipment. It appears that, like Arthur Schüller, he was being fast-tracked, doing his internship (Assistent) and his radiological research around the same time as Schüller. Even in those early years, Guido Holzknecht had recorded his conviction that every section of radiology required its own dedicated and expert specialists, in marked contrast to the views of the senior Professor of Surgery Anton von Eiselsberg who saw no need for too many specialties, including neurosurgery.

At the start of the twentieth century the General Hospital, or Allgemeine Krankenhaus, was a huge hospital of four thousand beds and numerous clinics. A number of small x-ray units had developed in individual clinics, but by 1902 these were transferred and consolidated into Nothnagel's x-ray facility, which became the central service provider of x-ray diagnostic services for the whole hospital, as well as the centre of radiological research.

By 1904, this had become the Central Röntgen Laboratory, situated in the Fourth Court of the General Hospital. Guido Holzknecht had already been occupied full-time for at least three years, concentrating on a wide range of body systems, particularly the radiology of lung disease. He was now seen as a future leader of the laboratory but was not confirmed as its director until 1905, probably awaiting his habilitation or higher academic qualification in 1904.

In 1902 Arthur Schüller began work under Holzknecht's direction in what was to become the Central Röntgen Laboratory; this became a warm and cooperative friendship until Holzknecht died prematurely in 1933.

Schüller remained in the Laboratory with the title of honorary research fellow for the rest of his career in Vienna, spending half of every day on his radiological research. He was not full-time or salaried and therefore probably never formally confirmed as a member of the x-ray department, in spite of being a valued and important part of its everyday intellectual life, in the process of which he acquired a vast knowledge of all aspects of radiology. Schüller's research in the laboratory rapidly made him the pre-eminent authority in the German-speaking world on the radiology of the skull and brain, particularly after the publication of his first two books, so much so that radiologists still held him in high esteem after generations of rapid technological advances.

He might well have become a full-time radiologist, had he been prepared to devote his efforts full-time, but he had other interests to pursue as well. In truth, he saw himself always as a neurologist first, a radiologist of the brain and nervous system, a discoverer of other diseases beyond the skull and brain, an experimental neurophysiologist, and finally something of an evangelist who threw off many ideas into other people's fields. In later life he confessed that he had been criticised by his friends in Vienna for spreading his activities too thinly and, as we shall see, his critics were to a certain extent correct.

⁂

When Schüller began his research in the Central Röntgen Laboratory in his early twenties, it was well recognised that x-rays had failed to image anything of the brain apart from calcification and very little detail in the bone calvarium. Even before the discovery of x-rays, autopsy studies had revealed pressure effects on the inner surface of the thicker skull bones of the vault.

The skull base was a daunting problem with all its complexities – unavoidable overlap of images, the paranasal sinuses and mastoid air cells, numerous foramina, canals, protuberances, fissures, grooves and plates – but it did carry some hope and opportunity for his work. He must have reflected on this and recalled that every neural structure and almost all blood vessels entered or left the cranial cavity through a foramen or a canal in the base of the skull; here were his opportunities to come closer to demonstrating disease processes in, or in relation to the brain.

He began working on the skull base in 1902, combining this with tuition in laboratory science, training as a neurologist and psychiatrist, and soon to include pediatric neurology. Two years later, a new trainee in radiology, Gottwald Schwartz, came to the Laboratory and later recalled his early encounters with Arthur Schüller. He described him as a "young neurologist interested in radiology of the nervous system, a very slender, very exact, almost pedantic scientist whom Holzknecht valued very highly and to whom all skull cases were referred. His diagnoses and reports were exceedingly short and precise."

Brevity and precision remained a hallmark of Schüller's reports until the end of his life; there was no need for a laborious expansion of the mental processes by which he reached the conclusion, unless challenged. Then, he was forthcoming with detail. The skull base was chosen, probably because of its complexity, which presented many opportunities for study and also because little systematic work had been done by his predecessors. Being Arthur, he was not slow to remind them of this in the introduction to his book on the subject published in 1905.

Research began with the construction of an apparatus for fixing and maintaining the head, living or skeletal, the x-ray tube and its central beam, with the photographic plate in the necessary relationships with each other. The early work was done with this apparatus resting on a bench, sometimes with the tube mounted vertically and the plate resting on the bench. He sat with his feet under the bench.

Schüller paid for this exposure with a lifetime of radiation dermatitis on the front of his thighs and dorsum of his feet; he had no toe nails, and later he became infertile. In time, the preferred technique was to fix the apparatus to the wall so that the living patient was more comfortable seated and the head more easily positioned. Dried skulls were used in the first phase of the research; normal subjects in the second. The aim for skull base radiology was to develop projections which minimised the volume of brain and calvarial bone to be traversed by the x-ray beam in order to reduce secondary scattered radiation (by the brain and bone) which compromised the radiological image of the target region in the skull base.

This amounted to a major difficulty. The quality of the picture was also threatened by the movement of the subject; holding the breath was not an option because the exposure time was too long. Complete immobilisation for the necessary time was often impossible. Arthur Schüller, on the suggestion of his collaborator Isaak Robinsohn, offset some of these difficulties by fixing two glass x-ray plates together with the emulsion sides in contact to reduce the exposure time and to produce two images with some stereoscopic function. The other principles in the making of an x-ray photograph had already been established by radiologists working in other parts of the body and were adopted as needed. The experimental plan was to use skulls from the museum, selected for their "apparent normal size and shape" to define the normal appearances. Objects and regions of interest were tagged with radio opaque material in the early stages; this helped to identify false shadows resulting from secondary radiation.

This early work was laborious and prolonged, but it meant that the neophyte radiologist was training himself in the identification of skull images, a skill that was unique to him. Many hours spent in repeated examination of difficult films would leave him with a mastery which none could match during his lifetime.

The normal established, Schüller moved on to a systematic exploration of the abnormal, beginning with congenital anomalies and malformations, some of which he clarified for the first time, and then disease states classified under the groupings of bone destructive lesions and bone proliferations. The work took half of each day for two years while he continued with his clinical duties and the animal research.

The paranasal sinuses were excluded from study of the skull base and the air containing cavities in the temporal bone were only allowed passing inclusion; they were ultimately left to E.G. Mayer, twenty years younger than Schüller, who produced a classic volume on the radiology of inflammatory disease of the middle ear and mastoid air cells. Arthur Schüller did not refer to his reasons for this exclusion, but presumably it was because infections of the sinuses and mastoid dominated the story at that time, and as a student of the nervous system they were of little to interest him. However, with the passage of time, these structures acquired considerable importance as the effects of intracranial tumours on them were recognised. Schüller then turned his full attention to these structures.

The bony protrusions from the inferior surface of the skull base offered little consolation with the limited technology of the times, but Schüller scrupulously identified and displayed all of them radiologically. The exits of the various canals were characterised, though some of the smaller ones were obscured by the overlay of multiple bone images. He did not abandon these canals but wrote about them from time to time, as late as 1937 remarking that they did not attract the interest of many radiologists.

The superior or internal surface of the skull base was a different matter. The great mass of the brain sits on this surface and the bone of the floors of the anterior and middle fossae are thin except for the upper surface of the petrous temporal bone and for a slight thickening of the lesser wing of the sphenoid. These thin areas bear deeper convolutional impressions than elsewhere. Schüller discovered that the pulsating cortex sometimes penetrated the bone completely in cases of chronic elevation of intracranial pressure, and basal fractures could be followed by small protrusions of the cerebral cortex into the deficiency, even when the intracranial pressure was normal. Importantly, these deficiencies could involve the walls of the paranasal sinuses and the mastoid air cells and middle ear, giving rise to escape of cerebrospinal fluid from the nose.

The most prominent feature, situated in almost the geographical centre of the skull base, was the sella rising up on the plinth of the sphenoid sinus. Schüller's obsession with the pituitary fossa lasted until his last writing days and gold came in the form of discovery. The floor of the skull was the laboratory in which Arthur worked out the science behind his art.

These early years of the century were filled with his laboratory and radiological investigations as well as his clinical duties in psychiatry and neurology. One might reasonably ask how he managed to do all this.

Part of the explanation is seen in the relative paucity of radiologic papers which he submitted to the journals prior to 1905 when all his effort was directed into completing his research and his first book, *The Skull Base on the Radiogram (Die Schädelbasis im Röntgenbilde: Archiv und Atlas der Normalen und Pathologische Anatomie)*. This book was the first systematic description of the radiology of the skull, and described both normal and pathologic anatomy. It became the definitive work on the subject for many decades. Included were a number of special projections of the skull base, based on Schüller's extensive knowledge, including "Schüller's view" (a lateral oblique projection to display the mastoid air cells).

Nevertheless, in those pre-war years he produced eight papers in clinical neurology and his first article on radiology and neurology; this last appears to have been delivered as a lecture at the annual general meeting of the Association of German Neurologists in 1914. The length of the paper suggests that it had been an invited lecture of some importance to the meeting. On this occasion he confidently informed his listeners that what he was doing was called Neuro-Röntgenologie, or now more familiarly Neuroradiology, as radiology has replaced Röntgenologie, certainly in English-speaking circles.

A few weeks before the publication of the book, Arthur Schüller and his collaborator, Isaak Robinsohn, published two short papers on the anatomy of the skull base and its radiology. This was characteristic of Arthur Schüller; he seemed to like the idea of a flyer to precede a larger work. On other occasions he did this by giving a brief presentation to the weekly meeting of the Medical Society in Vienna.

Compared to the external surface of the skull base, the internal surface is relatively featureless. The dominant feature is the foramen magnum, where the spinal cord exits the skull, but in front of it on the sphenoid wing lies a small cavern, the pituitary fossa.

In the nineteenth century and, as to be described, the early years of the twentieth century in Vienna, the pituitary gland became an item of significant interest. In 1886 Pierre Marie, a distinguished Parisian neurologist and co-founder (with Eduard Brissaud) of the journal *Revue Neurologique*, published a report of a woman with a long history of headaches and failure of vision. He noted that she suffered coarsening of the facial features, enlargement of her hands and feet and a number of other bodily abnormalities which he brought together and named acromegaly. The picture was completed by the discovery of a pituitary tumour at autopsy sometime later. In 1886, a diagnosis of a pituitary tumour could perhaps have been made before she died if the visual fields had been examined, but Marie makes no mention of them in his reports. X-rays would not have been a possibility, of course, before 1896 at the earliest.

At the beginning of the twentieth century, the Vienna Medical School moved significantly into the history of the pituitary problem. Five names come to the fore, namely Anton von Eiselsberg, Jacob Erdheim, Alfred Fröhlich, Oscar Hirsch and Arthur Schüller – all functioning in separate disciplines. There were others with an interest in the problem, not only in Vienna but scattered all over Europe and America. Each had a specific expertise to contribute, though they worked independently and were not officially gathered into a dedicated work group.

In Vienna, each worked in his own scholarly area, but under the Vienna system, inevitably in close geographic proximity. Weekly meetings, even daily at times, ensured at least some knowledge of what the others were doing. We can assume with some certainty that discussions occurred widely between individuals, if not actual collaboration. In his later years, Oscar Hirsch testified that Schüller and Erdheim certainly collaborated in linking post-mortem findings to the x-ray evidence.

The Viennese work was not done in isolation; other workers were active in many places, and their work was being published. Leading the field was Harvey Cushing at Johns Hopkins University; he had begun ongoing research on the pituitary problem in 1906, both in the clinic and the experimental laboratory, the results of which he published between 1906 and 1912. He collected his work in his book on the pituitary body, published in 1912, which included an analysis and summary of almost anything published by others with a bearing on the problem.

Erdheim had been studying the anatomy and pathology of the pituitary gland for several years and had divided the individual tumour cells into different categories on the basis of their staining properties in histological preparations. He added the staining characteristics of tumour cells in the pituitary gland to the studies on the normal gland by Carl Benda in Berlin. Eosinophilic cells in cases of Akromegalie (acromegaly) were the only constituents of pituitary tumours known to be associated with bodily changes at this time. In the normal pituitary gland, basophil cells had yet to be identified as a cause of Cushing's disease; indeed there was controversy about their role in any pituitary tumour. The introduction of x-rays of the sella or pituitary fossa, which enabled a definite diagnosis pre-operatively, provoked intense interest in the diagnosis of pituitary disease.

The need for surgical solutions was soon pressing. Victor Horsley (1904) in London and Fedor Krause (1905) in Berlin were the first to operate on a pituitary tumour; they chose a transcranial approach from above, which was daunting for those who were not seriously committed to the development of brain surgery by this method.

The Viennese answer to this was an approach from below the plane of the skull base, reaching the floor of the sella through the nasal sinus system. The first such procedure was developed by Hermann Schloffer on cadavers in the Institute of Anatomy in Vienna; it was later classified as the superior nasal approach by Cushing.

Between 1901 and 1907, Alfred Fröhlich in Vienna had studied a boy who progressed to adolescence over that period. When reviewed by Fröhlich at the age of sixteen, he had undergone profound changes; there were severe visual changes with abnormal visual fields; he was obese with a feminine distribution of fat and an absence of body hair; external genitalia had not developed and there was marked atrophy of the testes. Skull x-rays, made in 1907, demonstrated an expanded and partly destroyed sella. This settled the diagnosis. Biopsy showed that the cell type was uniformly chromophobe (indicating a particular type of pituitary tumour).

Fröhlich described the body changes as dystrophia adiposogenitalis, but Fröhlich's Syndrome soon became the internationally preferred name. It is a very rare illness, predominantly seen in males, and associated with reduced secretion of gonadotrophin-releasing hormone which causes severe retardation of the growth of the testes among other effects. Fröhlich described his case as an example of "pituitary tumour without acromegaly" and thus he had now established the existence of another type of pituitary tumour characterised by specific somatic changes.

The operation on Fröhlich's case was performed by von Eiselsberg in 1907, using a modification of Schloffer's technique. The so-called superior nasal approach from below the skull base was initially the choice of most European rhinologists and general surgeons, although Horsley and Krause continued using the transcranial approach. This approach through the nasal sinuses was especially preferred in Vienna where large numbers of these procedures were done in the next few years. Von Eiselsberg, the master general surgeon, reported two hundred personal cases. (There were no specialist neurosurgeons in Vienna at that time, and he saw no need for specialists in this area.) Both methods were dangerous in those early days, and the superior nasal approach, in its various forms, was both dangerous and mutilating.

There was need for a change in concept and technique, and it came in the idea for an inferior nasal approach to the sella, by way of the nasal cavity and the sphenoid sinus. This was presented to the Society of Physicians in Vienna by Oscar Hirsch in 1909. His senior colleague in rhinology, Professor Marcus Hajek, who was an expert on drainage of infections from the sphenoid sinus, thought that going further into the pituitary fossa would be too dangerous. This idea was also greeted with some scepticism by other senior clinicians, but Hirsch pressed on and performed the first operation in 1910. There was immediate interest among surgeons on both sides of the Atlantic, but in Vienna it seems that Hirsch's technique was not quickly adopted by his colleagues.

Nevertheless, it had caught the eye of the American competition.

Harvey Cushing had performed his first superior nasal approach in 1909 but abandoned it in October 1910 in favour of an inferior nasal approach, a modified version of the approach described by Allen Kanavel at Northwestern University in Chicago. After adding a further minor modification, Cushing's technique has been the most frequently used approach to this day, though it continues to be refined.

Cushing seems to have been undisturbed by the issue of priority and he simply refers to Hirsch as the forerunner of his own method. Hirsch continued to amass a large series of cases in Vienna until he left in 1938, settling in Boston USA.

The role of Schüller in precipitating these beginnings might seem controversial. He had not committed his ideas to the press at the time of Hirsch's proposal or first operation, but early in 1911 he published ideas that were based on a straight-line approach from the nostril to the sphenoid sinus, sella and third ventricle. This amounted to a number of radical proposals for the management of any intracranial tumour which presented with hydrocephalus as an emergency. He had also advocated removal of the floor of the sella alone to decompress an enlarging pituitary tumour and relieve the pressure on the optic chiasm (causing blindness) in those cases where further measures were thought to be dangerous.

In the 1940s, speaking to his friend Frank Morgan, he claimed that he had introduced Hirsch to the idea and had encouraged him to follow it. Morgan accepted this claim without question and promoted its cause wherever he went in professional circles at home and abroad. Arthur Schüller always mentioned the inferior nasal approach to the sella as one of the four conceptual surgical procedures for which he claimed priority. It is perhaps invidious to Hirsch and his memory to mention this story but its validity depends upon Arthur Schüller's reputation for integrity among his Australian colleagues. Indeed, this mention of the story comes from Frank Morgan's obituary for Schüller, which states that he had "commanded Hirsch" to do the operation in this way. It is hoped that this mention should not damage Oscar Hirsch's achievement and reputation or inappropriately increase Schüller's, but there may be truth to both their claims. Both men were working in the same hospital, the Franz Josef Ambulatorium in the Sixth District of Vienna, where they would see each other almost daily; and they were both part of the intimate and concentrated Vienna system of frequent meetings and discussions. When there is widespread activity in a particular area of medicine and surgery, the phenomenon of more than one person developing the same idea at the same time is almost inevitable.

Von Eiselsberg was the first to perform Schloffer's operation, and thereafter it became known as von Eiselsberg's operation in much of the English language literature. After all, he was the director of the clinic as well as being one of the most highly regarded surgeons on the international scene. He modified it during his early operations and the procedure became less mutilating in its final form; nevertheless it was still a formidable and dangerous procedure.

These events were followed by a slower-paced period of evolution. There was still much to do in explaining the functional relationships between brain, pituitary gland and soma; discovering and confirming all the details of the physiology would take more than fifty years to complete. The golden age of Vienna's romance with the pituitary problem ended in 1912 with two momentous events: Arthur Schüller published his masterwork on the radiology of the skull and brain, and Harvey Cushing published his masterwork on all aspects of the pituitary gland.

Schüller's book, *Röntgen-Diagnostik der Erkrankungen des Kopfes* (*Röntgen Diagnosis of Diseases of the Head*) encapsulated his extensive work and could plausibly only have been written by someone who was both a radiologist and a neurologist. This book became the standard textbook of neuroradiology for many years to come. Dr Fred Stocking, an American postgraduate student, translated it into English while studying with Schüller and some years later, in 1917, it was published by the US Army. Surprisingly, Stocking made no personal acknowledgment of the original author; Schüller's copy bears no inscription from the translator and the book does not include an introduction from the author. It appears to have had a limited circulation. Nevertheless, Schüller became the acknowledged expert in the field and increasingly clinicians from around the world came to Vienna to learn from the master.

With these two books and his lectures in the hospitals at which he worked, and tutorials after hours in his apartment, he taught a generation of physicians, surgeons and radiologists the intricacies of the skull. His excellent command of English (as well as French) and his reputation as a lecturer certainly aided his celebrity.

In 1924, a young Melbourne radiologist, John O'Sullivan, who was competent in German and French, attended his course in skull radiology. In the same year that Schüller published his book, Harvey Cushing, the great American neurosurgeon, visited the Vienna group and the two met. Arthur Schüller presented Cushing with a copy of his recently published work, and after returning to Baltimore, Harvey Cushing sent Schüller a copy of his own work. It was accompanied by a characteristically graceful letter which appears to be the only letter Arthur Schüller ever deliberately kept. During his visit to Vienna, Cushing also renewed his friendship with Alfred Fröhlich; the two had met in 1900 when they were both doing graduate studies in physiology with C.S. Sherrington in Liverpool. Their friendship was lifelong.

These days marked the end of Arthur Schüller's major contributions to the radiology of pituitary tumours. He had discovered all that was to be discovered in the plain radiography of the skull, at least in the opinion of Eric Lindgren in his authoritative history of neuroradiology. There were great technical advances to come, but the first of them was six years in the future in the form of ventriculography and encephalography, introduced by Schüller's friend-to-be, Walter Dandy.

Schüller was destined to be deprived of, or personally neglectful of, the opportunity to explore the possibilities of contrast radiography. Nevertheless, the world used his discoveries for routine radiography of the sella and its environs; the diagnosis of pituitary tumours then and for many years dependent upon a plain radiograph in the first instance. His radiological work on the sella and its environs remained the last word in the diagnostic process for the next six years until Dandy published his work on air ventriculography.

He remained the dominant influence in the education of graduate radiologists working in neuroradiology. They came from all over the world to Vienna to take his courses, as did general physicians, neurologists and surgeons, and of course his two books remained the final word on the normal and abnormal radiological appearances of the skull.

People who knew Schüller were aware of his claims that he was responsible for describing three diseases and at least three, possibly four, operations. The condition for which he is most recognised was probably the least important. In 1915, Schüller published a paper that forever made his reputation with medical students prone to learning about rare diseases with intriguing names (which they were never likely to encounter). He described the cases of two children, aged five and sixteen years, with hepato-splenomegaly, lymphadenopathy, diabetes insipidus and destructive bone lesions of the skull.

In 1919, Dr Henry Christian, Physician in Chief at the Peter Bent Brigham Hospital in Boston, described a case of extensive lytic lesions in the skull bones, exophthalmus and diabetes insipidus in a five-year-old girl. Dr Alfred Hand from the Philadelphia Children's Hospital had already described a case of a three-year-old with similar features in 1893, and much later, in 1921, surveyed the literature on the condition. From that time forward the condition came to be known as Hand Schüller Christian disease. Hand could only find the cases previously reported by himself, Christian and Schüller, and missed a case presented by Dr Thomas Kay in 1905, thereby denying

Kay his chance of immortality! Kay had correctly identified the hallmarks of the disease – exophthalmos, diabetes insipidus, and defects in the skull bones – known since that time as Kay's triad.

The other condition of greater significance, and for which Schüller certainly can claim precedence, is the condition osteoporosis circumscripta. In 1926 he described circumscribed osteoporosis of the skull bones in two cases and, in a strange twist of fate, one of the patients was biopsied by Harvey Cushing. The microscopic appearances were consistent with the early stages of Paget's disease of the skull, an explanation with which Schüller concurred.

In 1946, Schüller was the first to describe the appearances of calcified haematoma of the skull following injury suffered at the time of birth. He was the first to recognise the characteristic appearances of the skull bones as a consequence of chronic raised intracranial pressure and the importance of shift of a calcified pineal gland in localising intra-cerebral tumours. In a prescient work published in 1934, he introduced the concept of intra-cerebral localisation based on skull radiology (*Craniocerebral Diagrams for Radiological Localisation*) with Hubert Urban which set the foundations for current stereotactic intra-cerebral approaches.

Schüller also laid claims to describing the basis for at least three operations, although as a non-surgeon the validity of these claims is debatable. Nevertheless, based on his early research work in animals (1910) in response to the common problem of lightning pains in patients with advanced syphilis, he suggested the use of anterolateral cordotomy for intractable pain (as described above). Similarly, Schüller provided the anatomic basis for the trans-sphenoidal approach to the pituitary as described by Oskar Hirsch who did acknowledge Schüller's role, unlike Spiller and Martin, who, although aware of Schüller's work with respect to cordotomy, essentially dismissed it. He also suggested a posterior cisternal approach to drainage of the third ventricle for hydrocephalus, again well before it was actually performed.

From well before the start of the First World War, Schüller was recognised as one of the foremost experts in skull radiology. Difficult cases frequently made their way to him. He carried a heavy teaching load within the university, and there is some evidence he approached the university authorities after the First World War to promote the idea of postgraduate training, no doubt with the international fee-paying market in mind. Many clinicians from around the world made the pilgrimage to Vienna during the 1920s.

Two Australians who made the trip were subsequently to aid his passage to Melbourne. Hugh Devine, who was a surgeon with a particular interest in the upper gastrointestinal tract at St Vincent's Hospital in Melbourne, had visited Guido Holznecht, the pre-eminent expert on radiology of the gastrointestinal system at that time. John O'Sullivan, a young Australian radiologist who was studying in the UK, had spent three months there obtaining a diploma from the University of Vienna and was to become pivotal in Schüller's move to Melbourne.

Schüller's fame also guaranteed him invitations to meetings at medical centres around the world and he appears to have been a willing traveller. There was a busy schedule of meetings throughout Europe and visits to the United Kingdom. There was also at least one visit to the United States, where he lectured at major centres, including the Mayo Clinic and Johns Hopkins Hospital in 1926, as well as a visit to Argentina around that time.

In September 1967, ten years after Arthur Schüller's death, the neuroradiologists of the world met in Paris for the Eighth International Symposium Neuroradiologicum under the presidency of Herman Fischgold, the doyen of French neuroradiology.

The participants were given a small book entitled *A Short History of Neuroradiology*. The authors, Fischgold from Paris and James Bull from London, the doyen of British neuroradiology, confidently declared Arthur Schüller to have been the founder of neuroradiology. The front cover made clear their assessment of the pioneers in this field: they arranged photographs, in the temporal sequence of their contributions, of Arthur Schüller, Walter Dandy, Jean Sicard, Egas Moniz and Eric Lysholm. The photograph of Schüller was taken in his office, framing him in the doorway, at St Vincent's Hospital in Melbourne, Australia, in the mid-1940s, and given to Bull by the hospital neurosurgeon, Frank Morgan.

Bull had worked in neuroradiology in Stockholm in the 1930s under Erik Lysholm, where they became close friends. Bull subsequently named his department in the National Hospital for Nervous Diseases in London the Lysholm Department of Radiology. So he would have had good reason to support Lysholm's candidature for the founder of neuroradiology had that matter arisen, but he joined with Fischgold in declaring Arthur Schüller to be undoubtedly the founder of the discipline.

This appears to have gone unchallenged at the time; it seems not to have precipitated a response to the contrary in the English language radiological press. Previously, in his Presidential Address to the British Institute of Radiology in October 1960, James Bull had expressed the same opinion with equal conviction, also without adverse response. Much of the material in their book came directly from Bull's article and Frank Morgan's obituary of Schüller in 1958.

Another decade later the matter did arise when Erik Lindgren – Lysholm's successor in Stockholm – published an authoritative history, which made a powerful case for his choice, Erik Lysholm, as the legitimate founder of the discipline. In Lindgren's opinion, neuroradiology did not reach the point of formal definition until contrast radiology was developed. Lysholm did not invent ventriculography but there is no doubt that he established the principles and the technical apparatus which determined all skull and brain radiography thereafter.

Arthur Schüller's friend, Walter Dandy, invented ventriculography in 1918 and then encephalography in the next year, but he was a neurosurgeon who used his technique for his own purposes and in his own way in a very busy and innovative career, which probably explains why he failed to develop the radiologic aspects in detail. Further, the ideas and the technical apparatus to enable repeatable precision radiography had yet to come. This fell to Erik Lysholm.

Lindgren advanced his opinions while acknowledging the contrary belief of Bull and Fischgold. In this, as we have seen previously, he was more generous than those workers who had taken Schüller's ideas as their own after giving him scant recognition and dismissing his priority on flimsy grounds. Lindgren's justification for his choice of Lysholm as the founder of neuroradiology were based on a number of points.

Skull radiology is simply a subdivision of general radiology, which all radiologists are required to master. Lindgren sees it as a prodrome to neuroradiology and therefore dismisses any claim in support of Arthur Schüller as a pioneer of that discipline.

True neuroradiology begins only with the invention and application of contrast techniques which permitted, for the first time, the images of some brain structures other than those which show calcification. Lindgren believes that "at no time did Schüller express interest in the contrast medium studies that are the characteristics of true neuroradiology". While Lindgren is correct that Schüller was not involved at the outset with contrast studies, Schüller did later publish several articles based on this method.

Lysholm was the first person to produce the apparatus and the methods which allowed precise positioning of regions of interest within the cranial contents with respect to the central x-ray beam, and had the ability to repeat the exercise accurately. His principles changed the face of neuroradiology and carried forward the enormous development of the discipline from the early 1920s to the end of an era, which terminated with the arrival of computerised brain scanning in the early 1970s. No one would challenge Lysholm's status or contributions, or wish to do so.

Further, it is appropriate to add now to Lindgren's list that in the early 1930s, Lysholm unconsciously founded what came to be known as the Stockholm School of neuroradiology, which dominated the discipline for the next thirty years. This claim was not made by Lysholm himself; it was, however, made in 1995 by his successors Erik Lindgren and Torgny Greitz in the department Lysholm founded at the Karolinska Hospital. Few would disagree with the magnitude of his contribution.

In reality, both Schüller and Lysholm contributed significantly to the foundations of modern neuroradiology. Schüller's endeavours surely created the foundations for the extensive work of Lysholm and the Stockholm School, which in turn, supported by tremendous advances in technology, has led to the current state of high resolution CT scanning, MRI and interventional techniques in modern neuroradiology.

At worst, the efforts of Fischgold and Bull for Schüller, and Lindgren for Lysholm, can be viewed from a historical perspective as an acknowledgment and celebration of their respective mentors and friends. Whatever history judges, Schüller was the first person to introduce the term Neuro-Röntgenologie, or more familiarly neuroradiology.

The Skull Base on the Radiogram (Die Schädelbasis im Röntgenbilde: Archiv und Atlas der Normalen und Pathologische Anatomie) 1905 was Schüller's first book and a culmination of his early work on the radiology of the skull. Shown is the cover of Schüller's own well-worn copy he brought to Australia. He has written his name at the top-left and added St Vincent's Hospital on the right.

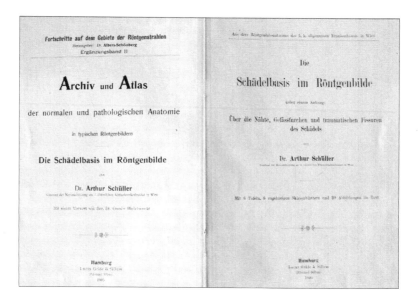

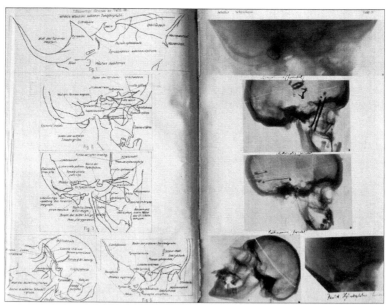

The Skull base on the Radiogram (Die Schädelbasis im Röntgenbilde: Archiv und Atlas der Normalen und Pathologische Anatomie). Shown are the front pages and a series of X rays reproduced as a photographic plate (printing was not up to the necessary resolution) with correlative diagrams.

The photographic plate has been further annotated by the author at a later date.

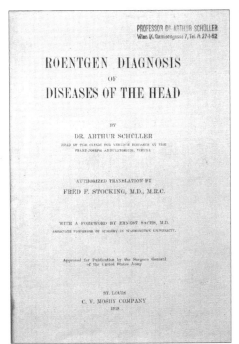

Title page of *Röntgen Diagnosis of Diseases of the Head*, Schüller and Stocking 1918. This book is a translation of Schüllers 1912 volume Rontgen-Diagnostik der Erkrankungen des Kopfes. This page is from the copy Schüller brought to Australia. Note the stamp with his home address and telephone number in Vienna.

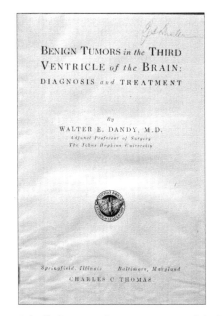

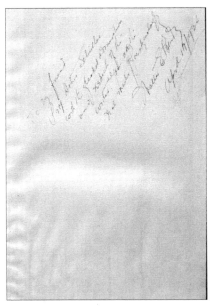

Schüller's copy of *Benign Tumors of the Third Ventricle* given to him by the author, his great friend Walter Dandy. Schüller brought this copy to Australia. It contains a warm message for Schüller on the fly leaf.

THE

PITUITARY BODY

AND ITS

DISORDERS

CLINICAL STATES
PRODUCED BY DISORDERS OF THE
HYPOPHYSIS CEREBRI

BY
HARVEY CUSHING, M.D.
ASSOCIATE PROFESSOR OF SURGERY THE JOHNS HOPKINS UNIVERSITY
PROFESSOR OF SURGERY (ELECT) HARVARD UNIVERSITY

AN AMPLIFICATION OF THE HARVEY LECTURE
FOR DECEMBER, 1910

319 ILLUSTRATIONS

PHILADELPHIA & LONDON
J. B. LIPPINCOTT COMPANY

Schüller's copy of *Pituitary Tumors* by Harvey Cushing given to him by the author. It was subsequently given to Frank Morgan by Schüller. It includes a warm letter from Cushing to Schüller.

HARVEY CUSHING, M. D.
107 EAST CHASE ST.
(COR. CALVERT)

BALTIMORE, July 24th, 1912.

Dear Dr. Schüller:-

I have returned to Baltimore, and wish to write you a word of further congratulation on your admirable volume dealing with the "Röntgen Diagnosis of Diseases of the Head." I have the more enjoyed reading it in view of the delightful and instructive hour that I passed with you during my recent stay in Vienna. I am taking the liberty of sending you, in return for your volume which you so kindly gave to me, a copy of a recent publication of my own dealing with the pituitary body question in general. I am ashamed to have you see many of the x-ray reproductions, but these cases represent some of my earlier ones, and the x-ray studies were very crude and insufficient. I am glad to say that we have been doing better during the last six months.

With regards, I am,

Most truly yours,

This letter from Harvey Cushing was one of the very few Schüller kept. It accompanied the book.

A SHORT HISTORY
OF NEURORADIOLOGY

by

Herman Fischgold and James Bull

VIIIth SYMPOSIUM NEURORADIOLOGICUM
September 1967

Title page of *A Short History of Neuroradiology* by Fishgold and Bull, given to participants at the Eighth International Symposium Neuroradiologicum in Paris in 1967. The photographs on the front cover listed the major players (from left to right) Arthur Schüller, Walter Dandy, Jean Sicard (upper panel), Egas Moniz and Eric Lysholm (lower panel).

Arthur Schüller and family on the occasion of his sixtieth birthday, 1934. Grete is to the right of Frederike Stiassni, Grete's mother, seated in front. Arthur is behind her and their two boys are to the right of both of them. Ernst and Alfred, Grete's brothers are probably in the back row.

Formal family portrait, 1934. Hans (right) was twenty-six and Franz (centre) was twenty-five.

Chapter Four

Without a Homeland – *Heimatlos*

I am thrice homeless,
as a native of Bohemia in Austria,
as an Austrian among Germans,
and as a Jew throughout the world.

– Gustav Mahler
(*Heimatlos*, quoted by his wife)

It was a tightly-held ambition of Adolf Hitler and the Nazi Party to form a greater German state which extended to all German speakers and their lands outside Germany. In Austria, demands by local pan-Germans became more vociferous as the 1930s came to an end, and at the same time German demands for Anschluss – the annexation of Austria into Germany – became more threatening. Finally, to resolve the issue the Austrian Chancellor, Kurt Schuschnigg, proposed a plebiscite to determine the fate of Austria. For strategic reasons Hitler was not prepared to let this occur; he demanded that power be handed over to the Austrian National Socialists or else Austria risked invasion. Faced with the inevitable, the Austrian government collapsed and Hitler's troops entered Austria without opposition on 12 March 1938.

On that same day, Heinrich Himmler, head of the SS, and Reinhard Heydrich, head of the Gestapo, arrived in Vienna to orchestrate the reception for Hitler and to commence the arrest of the political opposition. The next day, the German army moved into Vienna, after a halting progress across Austria, and with the army came the SS. Hitler went to Linz and stayed there until mid-morning on 14 March and then made a triumphant progress along the Danube towns, arriving in Vienna in the mid-afternoon.

Theodore Innitzer, formerly Professor of Theology in the university, later its Rector, and now the Cardinal Archbishop of Vienna, had arranged for all the church bells in Vienna to ring as Hitler entered the city.

The next day Hitler addressed a huge and enthusiastic crowd in the Heldenplatz from a balcony of the Hofburg, the Imperial Palace of the Habsburgs. He was accompanied by assorted dignitaries, including the Lord Mayor of Vienna and Archbishop Innitzer. Many in the square that day lived to regret their enthusiasm and some died as a consequence of it.

That evening Hitler had an audience with Innitzer at which the loyalty of Austria's Catholics was pledged. Some say Innitzer felt he had no alternative but to get onside with the Nazi authorities and play for time if he was to avoid some of the troubles experienced by the Church in Germany since 1933. The opposite view is that he was a convinced Nazi sympathiser or perhaps he thought them a solution to Austria's financial and political chaos.

Perhaps the real truth emerged three days later when the bishops of Austria signed pledges of loyalty, based on the conviction that Nazism would protect the nation against "godless Bolshevism which would destroy everything". Cardinal Innitzer added "Heil Hitler" to his own signature.

Confronted by what followed, he soon became an implacable opponent of the Nazis.

⁂

After Heldenplatz there was another day of relative quiet, and then came the thunderclap of popular anti-Semitism, ignited and spurred on by the SS. It exploded suddenly through the city, destroying Jewish property, throwing people out of their homes and physically assaulting Jewish people in the streets. Unspeakable humiliations were imposed on prominent citizens, some of whom were put to scrubbing pre-Anschluss anti-Nazi political slogans off the pavements with toothbrushes, surrounded by jeering crowds that included the regular German troops patrolling the streets.

The situation was too outrageous even for some of these soldiers and they intervened to protect the Jewish victims. Violent behaviour by the SS troubled even Reinhard Heydrich, Adolf Hitler's "man with an iron heart", the head of the SD (*Sicherheitsdienst*), the internal security force set up to oversee the SS. Heydrich's response to this chaos was to threaten to arrest any member of the SS who went too far.

After a few weeks, the frenzied violence settled down to a level of chronic and relentless persecution of Jewish people. In the meantime, the new government, under the control of Heinrich Himmler, was moving quickly, rounding up and imprisoning political opponents and other undesirables, and progressively implementing the introduction of the Nuremburg Laws, which had been designed to deprive Jewish people of their citizenship and all the associated privileges.

This spelt the end of the university positions of the Jewish professors and other university teachers who were all, technically speaking, civil servants appointed by the government. The mechanisms for their dismissal began almost at once. The process, decked out with "legalism", was deeply humiliating.

Eduard Pernkopf, the Professor of Anatomy and Director of the Anatomical Institute, had long been a very vocal member of the Austrian Nazi party and a member of the party's paramilitary *Sturm Abteilung* (SA or Stormtroopers), also known as the Brownshirts. He was immediately appointed provisional Dean of the Medical Faculty by Himmler himself.

On 6 April 1938 Pernkopf, clad in his Nazi SA uniform, called on the faculty to adopt Nazi ideals and policies in an address in the anatomy lecture theatre. He received the obeisance of his remaining faculty members. He purged the faculty of Jewish people and other academics deemed undesirable, and in the process the famous Vienna Medical School lost 153 of its professors and other senior researchers and an unknown number of more junior staff. It also lost almost half of its undergraduate medical students. Pernkopf, having drawn up the lists for dismissal, submitted them to the Rector of the university for formal approval.

Arthur Schüller and his Jewish colleagues received letters instructing them to prepare their genealogical credentials with a view to proving or disproving their race, according to the racial formulae of the Nuremberg Laws. Within a few weeks Pernkopf had been confirmed as the Dean and then, one by one, the academic staff were called before him, humiliated and dismissed.

Pernkopf had received a letter dated 22 April 1938 from the Ministry of Education containing the names of academic medical staff, including Schüller, to be "sent on holiday". In due course, Schüller was also discharged from the Children's Hospital and the Franz Joseph Ambulatorium as well. Pernkopf, on the other hand, had a meteoric rise. He became rector or chancellor of the university and continued to work on his anatomy textbook.

With the end of the war, he fled Vienna but was apprehended by US forces and was interred for nearly three years. On his return to Vienna, he continued his work on the anatomical atlas and was given space in the Institute of Neurology to continue his work. The Institute was, of course, where Arthur Schüller had worked prior to the war. To the university's everlasting discredit, the staff who had been dismissed by Pernkopf, if they survived, were actively discouraged from returning after the end of the war. Pernkopf's *Atlas of Anatomy*, almost universally regarded as one of the premier works in the genre, was to become infamous for another reason apart from the author's adherence to national socialism. The realisation that anatomical specimens used in the Institute of Anatomy and as subjects for the Atlas were obtained as a consequence of Nazi executions between 1938 and 1945 fired an ethical debate that continues to this day. The notoriety of the work eventually resulted in the publisher deleting it from their catalogue.

A massive program to eliminate all Jewish elements in the economy was ongoing in the *Alte Reich* (pre-Anschluss Germany) and it continued in the Ostmark, the new official term for Austria as a region of the new greater Germany. Appropriation or closing of businesses left many penniless. Later came restrictions on movement and on association with Aryans.

Schüller's private practice was restricted to treating only Jewish people. He was denied access to the city's parks and forbidden to appear on the streets with non-Jewish people. When Walter Dandy offered him financial assistance, he said that it was not needed. They kept out of trouble on the street, probably because they avoided the street for the most part, living in a substantial block of apartments with an entrance to a courtyard secured by high iron gates. The street level of the building was given over to small shopkeepers able to accommodate the residents' needs.

Nevertheless, the pressure on the now non-citizens to leave Austria was relentless, and those who could afford the exit tax and travel expenses, and were able to obtain entrance visas for other countries, left in numbers large enough to evoke the compassion of the international community and to alarm the governments of the countries which were the hoped-for destinations of the emigrants. Representatives of a group of concerned governments, thirty-two in all, including Australia, assembled under President Roosevelt's patronage.

In the event, Evian water is about all that came out of the Evian Conference. They met in the French resort town of Evian in July 1938, and one after another they recited a litany of reasons for agreeing to a very limited intake, if any, of Jewish immigrants. "They were still recovering economically from the Great Depression; they had serious unemployment; their constitutions did not permit altering the immigration quota in favour of any particular group; they feared that anti-Semitism would be stirred up in their peoples; they had housing shortages" and so on. All of the reasons were true, no doubt in some degree, but the failure of Evian sent a message of despair to the Jewish people of Austria.

They were now confronted by enormous difficulties, and many had little chance of escape. At best, they could be left impoverished, persecuted and always at risk of physical violence until the Germans were defeated, and they could not rely on that. Many died in the prisons and concentration camps where exhausting forced labour, random beatings and even summary executions claimed many lives. But as the routine extermination of Jewish people was more than two years away in 1938, and may well have been unforeseen at that time even by many in the upper levels of the Nazi government, there was still an element of hope of riding out the storm.

Many of Schüller's colleagues were quick to act before visas and offers of personal assistance began to diminish in the face of overwhelming numbers. From the Institute of Neurology, Benno Schlesinger had gone to Oxford even before the Anschluss, and Otto Marburg, the Director, to New York. His fellow members of the group who had made massive contributions to the study and treatment of pituitary tumours, Alfred Fröhlich and Oskar Hirsch, had gone to America early in 1938.

Arthur Schüller, very much a Viennese, swung between leaving and staying; although he never spoke of this, his correspondence indicates that he was exploring possibilities abroad from an early time, if not always with conviction.

His Stiassni in-laws agitated for immediate emigration, but they were cosmopolitan and experienced international business people, accustomed to moving around Europe, including Britain, and still secure citizens of an untouched Czechoslovakia. Alarmed by the looming prospect of German annexation of the Czech Sudeten lands, and perhaps worse, they were not inclined to wait on developments. Grete's brothers Alfred and Ernst set about moving their families and finances out of Czechoslovakia immediately. Two Stiassni nephews left as soon as possible; one flew his own aeroplane to England as the Germans entered Vienna. When the war came, he was interned on the Isle of Man as an enemy alien before his release to serve out the war as a pilot in the Royal Air Force. Grete's brother Alfred took his daughter Suzanne to England and placed her in boarding school; thereafter he had good reason to move back and forth between Czechoslovakia and England without exciting the suspicion of the Czech authorities in the process.

By then, the Czechoslovakian government had closed the borders against the movement of money and valuables out of the country. The two brothers with their families reached their final destination, New York, in September 1940 where the older brother Rudolf had previously taken up residence.

Frederike Stiassni, the matriarch, was taken to Switzerland but she became miserably homesick and insisted on returning to her friends and her home in Brno. She was prepared to die there.

After the Sudeten annexation on the first of October, Alfred, now in England, made a second desperate attempt to get her out, instructing his chauffeur in Czechoslovakia to drive her to Switzerland again. The rest of Czechoslovakia was now partly surrounded by a crescent of Germandom looking eastwards with menace. They were stopped at the new border between Czechoslovakia and the Sudeten territory and turned back. It was too late, and she remained in German hands for the rest of her life.

George Karpeles, the son of one of the Stiassni sisters, was arrested in Vienna soon after the Anschluss and sent to the Dachau concentration camp in Germany. Later he was returned to prison in Vienna and shortly thereafter released, after which he went to England.

Arthur's Schüller's cousins did not hesitate to follow the Stiassni example, moving out to England and America very soon after the Anschluss. Arthur, on the other hand, took a more Viennese approach to the turbulence in Central Europe and he seems to have been less worried, but there are clear signs that he was attaching some weight to the situation. Always publishing preferentially in German, he now began writing articles (regrettably lightweight) in English and submitting them to American and English radiological journals, where he had no lack of friends in editorial offices.

In December 1938, he told Dandy, who was urging him to come to America, of his preference for Australia, but reserved his final decision. Dandy, a giant of world neurosurgery and with influence in his own country, could not understand this. Schüller thought that he could do more in Australia to help his sons after the war and he specifically mentioned an interest in Brisbane. This may have been because he was aware that the University of Queensland had established the Brisbane medical school only in 1938, and he perhaps thought that there might well be opportunities there for senior scientists. He probably had contacts in Brisbane, perhaps someone who had come to Vienna for one of his courses. There has also been a suggestion that he had a cousin or other distant relative in Brisbane.

Dandy found the idea of migration to Australia as opposed to America somewhat bizarre, but Sigmund Freud and Julius Wagner-Jauregg, Schüller's mentor in his youth, would have disagreed. Some fifty years earlier, a year or two apart and independently, they had seriously considered moving to Australia shortly after graduation.

But there was another issue. Since 1933 there had been a constant flow of Jewish scientists and scholars into the American universities, leading to anxieties among the ranks of junior academics, who feared that their progress would be impeded by the lateral insertion of too many competitors from abroad, no matter how eminent. The unrest at Harvard University made its way into the press and Arthur attributed this to rising anti-Semitism; he told Walter Dandy that he was concerned that America was following in the footsteps of Europe in its anti-Semitic bias.

In fact, no country was without blemish. He had applied without success for admission to his native Moravia, then still part of Czechoslovakia and where his sons were actually citizens. In the letter to Dandy, he touched, in a surprisingly low-key way, on the difficulties he was having securing entry visas to other lands, and he commented upon the complex bureaucratic mechanisms operated by the SS in purging Austria of its Jewish people. This involved the investigation of, and granting of, political clearance, determining the appropriation of Jewish property, the exacting of the exit taxes and the replacement of Austrian passports by German documents.

⁂

On the 9 November 1938 there was an organised "spontaneous" pogrom which swept Germany and what used to be Austria in a terrible upsurge of destruction. Synagogues, houses and other properties were wrecked and burned, and their occupants dragged into the streets; many were beaten up, and not a few died as a result. This was *Kristallnacht* in Germany, better known by the Schüllers and others in Austria as Black Thursday.

It seems that this was the only occasion on which Arthur Schüller was subject to physical injury, and he mentioned it to Dandy in a surprisingly casual manner. The injury was probably minor; nevertheless it must have caused enormous distress and anxiety. But they were to endure far worse. Grete's sister Anna Tafler, a diabetic, was falsely denounced for a breach of the anti-Jewish laws and spent some days in prison without insulin. Her health never fully recovered. Desperate to get to Switzerland, she was smuggled past the Italian border authorities and given sanctuary in a Catholic convent hospital until a Swiss entrance visa was obtained with the assistance of her brother Rudolf, a long-time Swiss resident. She died a few months later.

Her adult daughter, profoundly deformed and disabled by juvenile rheumatoid arthritis, had married despite her disabilities. She and her husband could find no haven and they had to remain in Vienna. She later became a victim of the Nazi eugenics program, at that time using mobile carbon monoxide gas chambers mounted on trucks. An earlier death spared her mother the unimaginable agony of learning of this.

⁂

After Evian, the plight of Jewish people in Austria was desperate. The Viennese Jewish Cultural and Welfare Committee was seeking assistance from Jewish people and others all over the world, but with small returns. They had insufficient resources to assist those who had converted to Christianity, but they offered some help to baptised Jews who were prepared to re-embrace Judaism.

Schüller had no need of this; Hugh Cairns, the recently appointed Professor of Surgery in the University of Oxford, had invited him to come to Oxford, but, as he told Dandy, this was simply a transit arrangement and without long-term possibilities. Either way, it was an encouraging first step. Cairns, a neurosurgeon who had jointly written a book on neuroradiology, was well acquainted with Schüller's contributions and may have thought about appointing him to his department as a radiologist. The two had met when they both pre-sented papers in the same section on the same day at the International Conference of Neurology in London in 1935. There is no evidence to suggest that they had kept in contact thereafter and, at this stage of his life, Schüller was not publishing much work of interest to neuro-surgeons. Almost certainly, Cairns entered the field at the request of Schüller himself or of someone representing him, possibly the Society for the Protection of Science and Learning, or even Benno Schlesinger, the Viennese neuro-anatomist who was in Oxford on a Rockefeller Fellowship.

Many Jews could not afford the travel expenses and were thereby trapped. The Germans used some of the heavy exit taxation levied on the wealthy to help finance the exits of some less wealthy. This was no act of kindness, but in the words of Heydrich "to get rid of the Jewish mob". However, beyond that there was the problem of sponsors and entrance visas in other lands, and the numbers could not meet with the demand.

At one point the Schüllers decided to stay in Vienna and hope to survive by treating other Jewish people who were unable to leave. They were also prepared to die there. What led them to change their minds is unknown.

Not long after the Anschluss, Cardinal Innitzer began writing letters to bishops around the world seeking assistance for any of his congregants who had converted from Judaism and who were fortunate enough to reach their dioceses, but there is no evidence that Arthur ever presented his to the Archbishop of Melbourne. The need did not arise.

In December 1938 John McEwen, the Minister for the Interior, told the Australian Parliament that the government had decided to accept fifteen thousand refugees over the next three years, of whom five thousand would be Jewish people. Only some fifteen hundred Austrian Jewish people reached Australia before the outbreak of Second World War overtook the others, including the Schüllers' sons.

Earlier in the year, a secret meeting of the Federal Cabinet had discussed the issue, but nothing came of it. The Australian public was not without its concerns about the government policy; some of them were genuine anxieties and some were crude outrageous bigotry driven by the "yellow" press, with a range of views in between.

The small Jewish community, less than one per cent of the population, largely assimilated and relatively dispersed in the community, was fearful that an influx of Jewish refugees would exacerbate the low-level, largely veiled anti-Semitism. It was a rational fear and their leaders made a reasonable approach to the government, advocating caution, particularly in Sydney with its population of successful and well established Jewish people. This did not necessarily imply a rejection of the refugees, but the need for a measured and controlled response.

In retrospect, it seems that much of the rest of the world simply did not comprehend the magnitude of the problem or in some way shut their minds to it. At that time, the policy of mass extermination of Jewish people under German domination had not yet arisen. Special interest groups also spoke up, including the Australian branch of the British Medical Association (afterwards known as the

Australian Medical Association), which feared an impact on the virtual monopoly enjoyed by its members. Australian doctors were not alone; the President of the Royal College of Physicians (London) advised the British Home Secretary that there was likely a limited benefit for the nation from taking in the refugees because the number of German physicians and medical scientists who could teach British medicine anything could be numbered on the fingers of one hand!

Some time in January 1939, the Schüllers received their visas for Australia, but there remained a delay in processing their emigration. This was solved by a young lieutenant of the SS with a genius for organisation; he brought a number of separate departments involved in the mechanisms of emigration into a coordinated whole, reducing the process of ejection to one day. His name was Adolf Eichmann.

The Schüllers received their passports on 14 April 1939. They were described as "stateless" and in their passports their first names were followed by the second names then prescribed by the Nazi government for all Jewish people: Israel for men, Sarah for women. The documents were then stamped with a heavy capital J to facilitate the work of immigration authorities and border guards in other lands. This latter refinement was introduced in response to a request from the Swiss government, which was struggling under the weight of Jewish emigrants attempting to enter the country. The required "*Vermögensverzeichnis*" document, dated 15 July 1938 for Arthur and Grete, was a reckoning of the value of all their goods and chattels in order to determine the amount of the Jewish tax and the exit or "flight" tax, and a record of their payments. It is a poignant reminder of how much more they were about to lose.

A few days later Arthur Schüller left Vienna, a man forced out of his homeland, a homeless mendicant, and now thrust into bondage in an alien land, a bondage of dependency on people whom he did not know … *Heimatlos.*

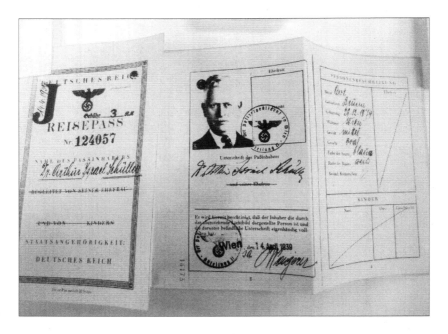

After the Anschluss, Austrian passports were no longer valid and were replaced with the German *Reisepass*. These documents were issued in April 1939. Arthur's middle name is recorded as Israel and Grete's as Sarah to signify that the bearers were Jewish. To leave absolutely no doubt as to the ethnicity of the bearer, the passports were also stamped with a large J (for *Juden*) at the request of the Swiss government, which had to manage large numbers of people coming across their border. (Australian National Archives)

Chapter Five

To Oxford and on to Melbourne

What I do now, is draw attention to the spirit of supportive collegiality.

– Barbara Falk

Caught in a Snare: Hitler's Refugee Academics 1933-1949

The Schüllers went to Oxford on the basis of an invitation from the Nuffield Professor of Surgery, Hugh Cairns. Cairns was an Adelaide graduate who had been trained by Harvey Cushing in the USA and had subsequently spent most of his professional career in the United Kingdom. He was widely regarded not only as a brilliant surgeon but also as a charismatic and generous individual. Cairns, it seems, had never visited Vienna but it is known for certain that he met Schüller in Stockholm in the early 1930s and subsequently at scientific meetings throughout Europe. Schüller had also made several visits to the United Kingdom prior to 1938, and this had provided ample opportunity to develop something more than a professional relationship.

The exact nature of the invitation, and what Schüller could expect in Oxford, is unknown, but there is a strong suggestion that he had already made up his mind to leave Europe. Cairns' invitation to Schüller was entirely typical of the man. Given the difficulties with employing senior foreign academics, particularly one within a few months of the mandatory retirement age of sixty-five, the invitation surely had a personal connection.

The path the Schüllers took from Vienna to Oxford is poorly documented, but Grete said that they had gone to Norway and then from Oslo to Britain. Many doubted this at the time but it is almost certainly correct. The number of Jewish people seeking emigration was increased by those caught in the Sudeten annexation, and it was becoming increasingly difficult for them to gain entry to the countries sharing borders with the new Germany.

The invasion of the rest of Czechoslovakia in 1939 meant another flood. Now it was virtually impossible to move out of German territory across any of its land borders, and it is well documented that people were forced to travel right across greater Germany from Vienna at the south-eastern extremity to the northern extremity where they could leave by sea from Bremen or Hamburg. It must have been an exhausting business, and there were risks both in exiting Germany and in gaining entry into another country.

On 17 August 1938, a group of Jewish refugees attempted to land in Helsinki, but they were too late. The Finnish Cabinet had closed the border to incoming Jewish people four days earlier because it was alarmed by the number of arrival visas which had been issued by their embassy in Vienna without prior permission from the government. This group of refugees were denied entry and the boat ordered to return to Germany.

It is possible that Arthur's and Grete's son Franz was involved in this voyage because of his familiarity with Finland. The Stiassni family believed this to be so. The families had always thought Franz a little eccentric because it was his habit to take his holidays each year with friends in Finland instead of Italy "like any sensible normal person". If he was in that group, he was returned to Germany.

In later life, Grete sadly reminisced to friends that their son Franz had accompanied them to Oslo, but she had sent him back to Czechoslovakia to attend to some financial matters, thereby sending him to his death. Nobody believed this as her mind often wandered in her last years; she likely confused a return from Oslo with the strong likelihood that Franz had been in the attempted Finnish landing and had to return rather from Helsinki. Franz might have been either in Vienna or Brno when his parents left in April 1939. By then Bohemia and Moravia had become German Protectorates (15 March 1939) and, as one family member remarked later, no one in their right mind would have tried to return, even if the Germans permitted it, unless driven by some extreme circumstance.

Franz, who had lived with his grandmother since his mid-teens, was deeply attached to her and this might have been that circumstance. But on balance, we may conclude that the boys remained in Brno for whatever reasons or returned there. Documents indicate Prague was Franz's last address before deportation to Terezín (Theresienstadt) and eventually Auschwitz.

Hans (incarcerated 4 April 1942) and his wife and daughter (both incarcerated 31 March 1942) were transported from Brno to Terezín. The Morgan obituary claims that the two boys were prevented from leaving Vienna at the last minute but this is clearly a misconception. The one certainty is that the Schüllers did reach Oxford without their sons and that they would never see or hear from them again.

Schüller was immediately invited into the scholarly haven of the Nuffield Institute for Medical Research where his friend Alfred Barclay, the academic doyen of British radiology, had arranged a position for him. This was to be his base for the next two months. Barclay and Schüller knew each other well, both enjoying the reputation of never missing an international radiology meeting in Europe.

It seems clear that Schüller did not ask for assistance then to remain in England, but viewed this position, that Cairns had set up with Barclay, as a staging post. Schüller was not on the university payroll and his name does not appear in the archives of the university or in the records of the Society for the Protection of Science and Learning (SPSL). The SPSL was set up in 1933, under a different name originally, with the aim of helping displaced academics into

British universities. The aims of this society restricted their capacity to be of much help to Arthur Schüller because, only a few months short of retirement age, it would have been virtually impossible for them to find a position or university finance for him. He must have known this.

⚬᪥᪥⚬

In his later years Schüller spoke warmly of his time at the Nuffield Institute; the university professor was at home among his distinguished peers. He certainly lost no time in settling in. Professor Wilfrid Le Gros Clark gave him facilities in the Department of Anatomy to continue his research in the radiological demonstration of the subarachnoid cisterns at the base of the brain. This work led to a publication in the British Journal of Radiology, and in it, Schüller acknowledged his indebtedness to the Nuffield Institute, Barclay and Le Gros Clark. His young colleague from the Institute of Neurology in Vienna, Benno Schlesinger, was already working in Le Gros Clark's department, supported by a Rockefeller Fellowship. He remained on as a member of the department after the fellowship expired, and after the war moved to America.

From the beginning, Cairns made Schüller part of all the activities of the Nuffield Department of Surgery, which was devoted entirely to neurosurgery, and he moved easily between it and the Nuffield Institute, less than a hundred metres away. He saw little of Hugh Cairns because Cairns spent much of his time in London advising the government on surgical services for the impending war, only a few weeks away, as well as developing and directing the head injury services for the British Army. The work of the department was left largely to Cairns' First Assistant, Joe Pennybacker, a young American who had trained in both neurology and neurosurgery in London, and who was rapidly making a reputation as a master surgeon and a brilliant diagnostician.

Schüller was captivated by Pennybacker's talents and personality, and the overall quality of the department, which was clearly superior to the neurosurgery in Vienna at that time. He mentioned this later to Australian colleagues more than once.[2] Hugh Cairns, a man of relentless energy, was assisting the SPSL and other organisations helping displaced scientists. Francis Schiller, a neurologist from Prague, was taken into his unit as a house surgeon and research assistant, and he placed a young Viennese neuropathologist, Eugen Pollak, with his colleague Geoffrey Jefferson in Manchester.

The Spanish Civil War produced a different group of refugees, among whom was Pio del Rio Hortega, arguably the most prominent histologist of the brain of his time. Cairns installed him as the neuropathologist in his department. Arthur Schüller saw him as a comrade in adversity, but the sad and depressed del Rio Hortega showed little interest in a friendship.

By inviting Schüller to Oxford, Cairns had begun the chain of welcome and support which landed the Schüllers in Melbourne three months later. They had probably abandoned the Brisbane plan before going to Oxford but, if not, they were now turned elsewhere by a consortium from Melbourne who all had their connections to Oxford and two of whom had direct experience of Schüller. Cairns had trained Frank Morgan, the first neurosurgeon at St Vincent's Hospital, and they kept in contact. Barclay had a special relationship with John O'Sullivan, who was the senior radiologist at the same hospital. O'Sullivan had spent the middle years of the 1920s in England studying and working; he took a course for the Cambridge Diploma of Diagnostic Radiology and Medical Electrology and then submitted himself for the examination. He achieved a perfect score, and the chairman of the board of examiners – Barclay – refused to believe that he had not cheated; he was required to take the examination again with a completely new set of unrelated questions. Again a perfect score. Barclay promptly gave O'Sullivan a job in his own department and later promoted him to assistant radiologist.

Not surprisingly, this was the beginning of a friendship between the two which continued over time; years later when O'Sullivan was in an executive position in the Royal Australasian Association of Radiologists, he secured the services of Barclay as the official representative of the Association at the British Institute of Radiology. O'Sullivan also knew Schüller; he had met him in 1924 and 1927 in Vienna when attending his courses on skull radiology, but had not maintained a correspondence with him afterwards.

Both O'Sullivan and Morgan, in frequent correspondence with their Oxford mentors, were anxious to help and surely, were not entirely unmindful of the prize they would bring to their city, hospital and departments.

The final Melbourne connection to Oxford and Schüller was Sydney Sunderland, the newly appointed Professor of Anatomy in the University of Melbourne. Schüller met him in Le Gros Clark's department, where Sunderland was completing a period of research. They both left Oxford for Melbourne at about the same time, Sunderland to visit America on the way.[3] In Melbourne they were to meet again as colleagues when Sunderland, after consolidating his new role, offered Schüller an unsalaried research position in his department in 1941.

While the other two members of the Melbourne consortium no doubt played their roles, it seems that it was John O'Sullivan who was primarily responsible for the process that brought Arthur to his new country and his new professional life. Around St Vincent's Hospital, the sense was that John O'Sullivan and Frank Morgan were jointly responsible. The full details can never be known for certain now, but the legend at least over-simplifies their respective roles. A more mature assessment of the available information, and discussion with the few remaining persons who knew Schüller at St Vincent's Hospital, gives the central role to O'Sullivan.

Brian Egan, in his masterful history of St Vincent's Hospital, came to a similar conclusion as the author on this point. Despite the serendipitous meeting of Schüller and Sydney Sunderland, in Le Gros Clark's Anatomy Department in Oxford, the timing and location would have made it difficult, if not impossible, for Sunderland to have negotiated the necessary arrangements. Obtaining a visa for

Australia took some months and almost certainly required support from someone in Australia at the time. Two names appear on the Schüller's arrival documents, a Mr Harald S Nettheim of Brisbane and Dr Edward Prendergast of Melbourne. Netheim, a stockbroker had met Schüller eleven years earlier in Cairo but nothing is known of the connection with Dr Prendergast. It was believed that Schüller had a cousin in Brisbane but it is not known if he and Nettheim were related or even knew each other.

Furthermore, Schüller was able to commence work at St Vincent's Hospital within a very short period of time after his arrival. Not only was Schüller's new position, irregular as it was, ready for him when he arrived, so were the critical financial arrangements. O'Sullivan is probably the only one who could have set these things in place; in 1939, he was head of the radiology department and a senior clinician around the hospital. He was clearly in a position to assist Schüller; this behaviour was entirely consistent with a man who was known for his great generosity and passionate commitment to social justice.

As we have seen, O'Sullivan and Barclay appear to have stayed in touch during the years before the war. Barclay may have had a hand in re-establishing contact between Schüller and O'Sullivan, who had reportedly not been in contact since O'Sullivan attended Schüller's courses in Vienna years earlier. On the other hand Frank Morgan had only returned from London three years earlier to become the hospital's first neurosurgeon. In 1939, he was still a relatively junior member of the senior medical staff, and as such not in a position to materially influence the hospital hierarchy. Morgan had not met him prior to his arrival in Melbourne, and may not have been familiar with the extent of work produced by Schüller. Nearly all of Schüller's publications to that time were in German, and as Morgan had trained in the United Kingdom he had received limited exposure to this literature.

The likely scenario is that Schüller had already decided on a move to Australia, and this decision was reinforced by the offer that came from O'Sullivan who was likely made aware of the Schüllers and their desire to move to Australia through his contacts in the UK. Frank

Morgan, once he became aware of Schüller's arrival, understood the importance of such a prominent neuroradiologist to the neurosurgical unit at St Vincent's which was less than a handful of years old and became highly supportive.

Arthur Schüller left one last mark before leaving Europe. Some time in 1938, a meeting of experts in the radiology of the skull and brain was arranged for the summer of 1939 in Antwerp. They aimed to establish international meetings of the group on a regular basis in the future. The two giant figures of the day were Schüller and Eric Lysholm of Stockholm, around whom were grouped some fifty radiologists from Britain, France, Germany, Holland, Italy and the Scandinavian countries, all by invitation.

On 23 July 1939, Arthur crossed to Antwerp for his last contact with continental Europe. The meeting ran from 24 to 28 July, and Schüller gave three papers, two in French and one in English. Characteristic of him was his desire to have his friend Walter Dandy included in the list of distinguished clinicians, and he sought Dandy's approval to nominate him for membership of this new association. Dandy agreed but in the event he did not attend, which is not surprising given the state of the world in July 1939. This was essentially a European exercise, and even though similar moves were afoot in America (and separately in Italy) at about that time, this meeting marked the beginning of a truly international forum.

When the neuroradiologists of the world met in an international forum in Rotterdam to form the Second Symposium Neuroradiologicum in 1949, they unanimously declared the Antwerp meeting to have been the first.

At the end of the 1939 meeting came the inevitable group photograph. Schüller was placed in the middle of the front row. Arthur Schüller stood with his head bowed and turned away from the camera, his hands clasped loosely in front of him, but he stood erect.

From Antwerp, Schüller went back to Oxford and then to London and onward to Australia. He never returned to Europe. Schüller spoke only sparingly of his reasons for coming to Australia. A dominant theme, however, was that Europe had failed him twice. Personally, professionally and financially, he had been devastated by the First World War, and the prospect of another war supercharged with the racial overtones of national socialism was enough for him to quit the Old World for the New. Why he chose Australia rather than the US, particularly as he had a standing invitation from his great friend Walter Dandy, has never been satisfactorily explained. But there was always a hint, as with many others who fled Europe around this time, of the desire to get as far away as possible.

Some who knew Schüller well suggested, with half a grain of truth, that he loved the grand symbolic gesture, but all would agree that he was a rigorous thinker who made his decisions logically and without emotion.

Antwerp 24-28 July 1939, meeting of European Neuroradiologists. Schüller is on the top step towering over his colleagues. In 1946 at the Symposium Neuroradiologicum, this Antwerp meeting in 1939 was acclaimed as the First Symposium Neuroradioligicum.

Dr John O'Sullivan, Radiologist, St Vincent's Hospital Melbourne. O'Sullivan more than anyone else was responsible for getting Schüller to St Vincent's and then supported him during the early years of his time in Melbourne.

A formal portrait of Frank Morgan, taken in the old Neurosurgical Unit office, St Vincent's Hospital Melbourne; the microscope was an instrument with which he had little familiarity. The picture out of focus on the wall immediately behind Morgan is Julian Smith's portrait of Arthur Schüller.

Chapter Six

Hospital

The Schüllers left England from Croydon Airport in south London by KLM airliner on a once per week service to Batavia in the Dutch East Indies, which had recently been extended to Sydney. The precise date is unknown but it is thought that the journey took five days, arriving in Darwin on 8 August 1939 after a multitude of refuelling stops; and it seems that most of the flying was done by day only.

The Schüllers went through the immigration formalities in Darwin, where they would have been required to pay an entry tax if it had not been paid in April when their visas were issued by the Australian authorities in Vienna. This tax was set at twice the level of that required of other immigrants because they were Jews, which implied that they would have more difficulty than others in obtaining employment and therefore be an extra burden on the country; they could never escape special attention.

There followed another day flying before they arrived in Sydney on 9 August.

⁕

It must have been a tiring and uncomfortable journey; they travelled in a Lockheed Electra, a twin-engined aircraft of modest size capable of carrying fifteen to twenty passengers depending upon circumstances, with a reputation for very high engine noise. The cabin was

101

not pressurised and they must have consumed a lot of barley sugar in the process of ascending and descending, to judge by common airline practice at the time. There is anecdotal evidence the Schüllers visited Brisbane, most likely on the trip from Darwin to Sydney, which required two refuelling stops, presumably to visit a distant family member (a cousin of Arthur) or one of their sponsors, Mr Nettheim. The local papers noted the arrival of the respected doctor.

The Schüllers remained in Sydney only a few days, almost certainly in contact with friends who had gone before them, before moving on to Melbourne in the State of Victoria. It is believed that they found an apartment almost immediately in the south-eastern suburb of Prahran on the border with the adjacent suburb of St Kilda, where many of the Jewish middle-class had settled over many years, which suggests that they had Jewish friends waiting to help them.

From that time until they bought their own house in 1950, they lived in an apartment in a subdivided and unprepossessing old house at 162 Punt Road. This meant that it took a bus journey followed by a tram journey in order to get to Arthur's new location at St Vincent's Hospital, but the bus and tram routes intersected and it was door-to-door at each end. Arthur Schüller was no stranger to public transport; he could not drive a car and had never owned one, either walking to his Viennese hospitals or taking a tram. This was routine for most people in Vienna, particularly in the inner suburbs frequented by the academic, legal and medical upper-middle-class, the majority of whom lived centrally in rented apartments.

John O'Sullivan and Frank Morgan left no stories behind them and no written records of Arthur Schüller's first meeting with them. They had arranged his appointment with the Sisters of Charity, who owned and operated St Vincent's Hospital and who would certainly have invited him. This ageing man then found himself in an alien culture, far removed from the high culture of Vienna, though perhaps with some sense of relief and security at last. It must have been a difficult business for him meeting the people who had rescued him and to whom he would have experienced something of a mendicant's gratitude, mixed with the knowledge that both he and they clearly recognised that he was the international master bringing great benefits to the hospital and to Australian radiology.

Regrettably, the latter was never fully realised. Add to this the humiliation of being required to report regularly to the local police station, in accordance with their classification as Refugee Aliens, which had been imposed upon them on the outbreak of the Second World War on 3 September 1939. As a member of the British Empire, Australia declared war on Germany automatically with the British declaration. There were no restrictions on the Schüller's civil liberties.

Presumably, if the arrangements for his appointment had not been negotiated by mail in advance, they were worked out now. Schüller's presence in the hospital tells us a lot about that institution. Already almost five years past retiring age from the teaching hospitals in Melbourne in those days and in which all senior medical staff were honorary, what was to be done with him? He was simply quietly installed in the x-ray department without fanfare; his name never appeared on committee minutes, annual reports or appointment documents and he was paid a modest sum from the collective budget for radiographers.

Arthur found in St Vincent's Hospital a small department but with modern equipment which would have differed little from that to which he had been accustomed; almost all of it had been imported from Britain, Europe or America and was of basic international standard for the times. The department was located in a new wing which had been built and equipped only four years earlier. It lacked a specialised Lysholm skull table, but Schüller had never enjoyed the luxury of using one in the finance-starved Vienna of the First Republic.

The staff took some pride in its heritage; its first director had been Dr Herbert Hewlett, who was the second medical graduate in Victoria to devote himself full-time to radiology. The Antoine Béclère Centre in Paris, after collecting evidence, pronounced Hewlett to be the first radiologist in Melbourne, but he made no claim for himself. Subsequently the Béclère Centre corrected its assessment in favour of Dr FJ Clendinnen and and left Hewlett honoured as one of the pioneers.

John O'Sullivan succeeded Hewlett as the second director in the mid-1930s. Australia had embraced the discovery of x-rays at about the same time as the rest of the world, which is not surprising given the utterly dramatic nature of the discovery. The first x-ray picture made in Australia was reported by TJ Lyle, the Professor of Physics in the University of Melbourne, and the first report on the use of x-ray in diagnosis came from Father Joseph Slattery, a Catholic priest of the Vincentian Order and head of the science department at St Stanislaus College in Bathurst NSW; an image was made of an injured hand at the request of a local general practitioner.[4]

The plan which was put to Arthur Schüller, and accepted, proved to be remarkably successful; he was to be based in the x-ray department, which was logical enough, but also invited to be part of the neuro-surgical unit. From the beginning, he was invited to take charge of all radiology concerned with skull and brain, but for legal reasons his reports had to be typed up and issued in the name of one of the two senior radiologists. This restriction persisted until he was registered as a medical practitioner with the State Health Department at the end of the war.

Schüller came almost immediately to the hospital and was received in the x-ray department with enthusiasm and much deference, where a flying start awaited him in the form of skull films of a man with a large bony lump in the frontal region. The diagnosis was pronounced to be an ossified cephalhaematoma, in an unusual position, dating from childhood. The professor immediately wrote this up in a case report submitted to the *British Journal of Radiology*. It was published immediately, in spite of the lack of biopsy and the presence of irregular thickening of the inner surface of the frontal bone and an abnormal development of the frontal sinus. He was probably aware that he had a friend at court; the honorary editor of the journal at that time was Dr Peter Kerley, a friend of John O'Sullivan. Kerley had accompanied O'Sullivan to one of Schüller's courses in Vienna during the 1920s.

News of Arthur Schüller's presence in Melbourne spread rapidly to the local radiologists, and he was given an enthusiastic welcome. He was invited to give several lectures to them, but after that the distractions of the war diverted their attention and he did not speak to the group again. Nevertheless, he exerted a genuine influence through the practice of individual radiologists bringing their problem films to him for advice. A history of radiology in the State of Victoria, written by Dr Malcolm McEwan, expresses the opinion "that Australian radiology was much in Schüller's debt".

The professor's expertise as a violinist was quickly discovered by the junior medical staff and he was recruited thereafter to provide an item in the annual Christmas concert put on by them. In some years his enthusiasm for following a tune with a lengthy series of variations of his own devising caused the producer some anxiety.

In the department Schüller was given a place at a bench running along the wall of a long narrow room where the visiting radiologists sat in front of a row of viewing boxes reporting the films. This room was as close as it came to the provision of offices for the radiologists. He sat among them or at one end. Initially he lacked the dignity of a personal office which a person of his status would normally command, but he was in the right place here where there was plenty of friendship, conversation with his peers, exchange of ideas and opportunity for advanced teaching. At that time he seemed happy in his new environment, and he moved about the department without reticence. The department rejoiced in a tea room with two or three leather padded armchairs where he could rest if necessary and conduct social niceties.

It seems that he was not formally involved in the teaching of medical students; in those days little was done in that regard by radiologists, but he was available to any of the students ferreting around the department working up cases in the wards. Indeed, he moved about the department looking for teaching opportunities with them and the radiology trainers.

One of the students in his later years recalled puzzling over the chest film of an obscure case, when an unfamiliar voice with an accent came from behind and announced the diagnosis to be pulmonary sarcoidosis. Schüller then delivered a superb tutorial on the differential diagnosis.

In his early hospital years the professor was always anxious to encounter the young. He took his lunch in the hospital cafeteria where he preferred to sit among the medical students, engaging them in conversation. But the sense of being a stranger followed him always.

There was a small dining room for senior medical staff off the cafeteria which was used almost exclusively by the laboratory scientists who worked full-time; clinicians for the most part gave their service in half-day segments, and they did not eat in the hospital. If Arthur Schüller was invited into the senior dining room it is probable that he did not accept it; it is equally probable that the laboratory scientists had never heard of him, working as they did in a building separate from the wards.

It appeared to most observers at the time that Arthur Schüller was settled and universally accepted and admired by the hospital community. Nevertheless, his presence in the hospital could be questioned. Here was a man who was already only a few weeks away from his sixty-fifth birthday, working in a hospital where the official retiring age for senior medical staff in those days, as in the other university teaching hospitals, was sixty. Many before him in this and other departments and hospitals had departed reluctantly at this age and there was a risk that what appeared to be special treatment for Arthur Schüller could be resented by someone and even voiced in public.

Furthermore, he had no private practice in the city and thus no obvious means of support, which would lead to the speculation that he was being paid for his services while all other senior staff worked without financial reward. This would be a breach of the honorary system and likely to attract notice among the health bureaucracy.

Besides, he was not eligible for registration as a medical practitioner in the State of Victoria where the Medical Board was accustomed to dealing only with graduates from institutions in Australia and Britain and elsewhere in the British Empire. Beyond this, the Board did have a list of approved institutions abroad. In a bizarre omission, the medical school of the University of Vienna was not on it! Almost certainly the medical board would not have had legal authority to grant Arthur Schüller a licence to practise. The country was preoccupied with the Second World War, which had just been declared, and this was no time to start drawing up lists of foreign medical schools and universities, particularly those now in enemy countries.

Discreet enquiry by John O'Sullivan to the Board on Schüller's behalf revealed that an application would fail and his advisers thought it best not to risk another humiliation for him. That would have to wait until the end of the war.

Anxious to explore all avenues, and before he had met Morgan and O'Sullivan, Arthur Schüller had lodged an application in Sydney with the medical board of New South Wales, which was better prepared than the Victorian model. Registration was granted in July 1941, and in May 1942 he was granted a licence to practise by the Commonwealth Government Health Department, but terms and conditions were not specified and the present day Health Department knows nothing of it. The license certificate remains in the Schüller archive.

However, he was well settled in Victoria by then and he decided to remain. Nevertheless, he was taking no chances and he paid the annual fee to maintain his New South Wales registration until shortly before his death, long after he had been granted citizenship. It seems that he never lost the sense of "otherness" which haunted so many others who had fled Europe. By remaining in Melbourne he had accepted that he would not be permitted to treat patients but he could undertake consultations referred by other practitioners and provide them with diagnostic and therapeutic advice.

The immediate need was to secure a subsistence income which was reliable. A member of the senior medical staff gave him free access to his consulting rooms at 33 Collins Street in the city after 4 pm in the afternoons, but that attracted very little in the way of referrals; mostly it was the occasional neurologic dilemma sent to Schüller by Frank Morgan and a small handful of other clinicians, mostly members of the hospital staff.

On one such occasion a woman was brought to his rooms by the referring doctor, who observed the examination. When this was completed, the professor seemed to be unsatisfied and when she was again fully clothed he took this astonished woman in his arms and, humming a Viennese waltz, took her for a turn around the room and then announced with satisfaction "yes, this is a cerebellar lesion". There was more intimacy in Viennese neurology than in Australia, as the professor found out on a ward round when he raised some questions to do with sexual function at the bedside, only to receive a sharp reprimand from Frank Morgan. Both parties were offended and there was a temporary rift.

Unfortunately, the income from this practice was insufficient and he began giving tutorials on skull radiology in his home at night and charging a small fee for them; this was directed at the radiological registrars who were happy enough to pay, but some of the elders in the profession, accustomed to the tradition of free teaching of under-graduate and postgraduate students in medicine, frowned upon this. This was probably Schüller's first cultural challenge, but it did not amount to anything serious.

Much more to the point was the situation which arose when a Sydney neurosurgeon came down to Melbourne to take a course from Schüller in neuroradiology and then arranged for him to come to Sydney and repeat the course at the surgeon's teaching hospital. After the event, Schüller charged a fee, a so-called honorarium for these services in line with normal practice in Vienna; it is not known whether it involved the hospital as well as the surgeon but certainly the surgeon rejected payment for his moiety, probably because it was contrary to the cultural practices in Australia at the time.

Looking back on this, it is hard to understand the neurosurgeon's attitude; he was a highly intelligent man, a well-to-do and much travelled cosmopolitan who should have been sympathetic to the professor's situation. After repeated attempts to resolve the issue, Schüller asked a young nephew of his wife who had recently migrated to Sydney to hand in the account to the surgeon's office in Macquarie Street and to wait until he was paid.

The result was disastrous; the enraged doctor stormed out of his consulting room into the waiting room containing patients and berated the youth, who left in a state of confusion and humiliation. He never forgave Arthur for putting him in this situation though he remained in contact with his aunt, but he did bring to Schüller the message that the doctor concerned was due to attend a meeting of the Neurosurgical Society in Melbourne in a month or two and that he would settle with Schüller then; he did not attend the meeting. If there was an outcome it is now unknown.

This regrettable episode did not occur until shortly after the end of the war, but right from the beginning it had been clear that the Schüllers had limited means for survival.

The solution to this dilemma was simple and direct; in the words years later of the hospital's official historian, Dr Bryan Egan, it said something about the Sisters who owned and operated the hospital. Religious orders are usually expert at discreet arrangements in the service of the Lord and those in need, and this was no exception. Quite simply, Arthur Schüller was never "officially" appointed to the medical staff of St Vincent's Hospital, his name did not appear on staff lists, hospital committees or Board minutes. A stipend of unknown size was excised from the officially approved budget for the radiographers, who were not individually costed or named in published staff lists. If the State Government Health Department knew about this, they presumably had no objection.

The professor remained at the hospital until failing health forced him to withdraw in 1956. There was never any expectation that there would be an official endpoint to his appointment. His presence in the hospital and in the hearts of those working around him was always accepted as the desirable norm.

There may have been another source of finance but if so, it was well concealed from the hospital community. In February 1942 Sydney Sunderland offered Schüller an honorary appointment as a research fellow in the Department of Anatomy. He did no formal teaching of undergraduates in the Anatomy School, but the students were quick to discover his presence there; the Medical Students Society invited him to give lectures but it appears that only one was delivered, in 1942, on the history of cordotomy. For some years he attended the department for one day a week.

Sunderland's department had an interest in anthropology, and this set Schüller about pursuing his long-held particular interest in the possibility of defining race and ethnicity, including the effects of ethnic cultures such as nurture on the morphology and metrics of the skull. For instance, he believed that the southern Slavs moulded the head of a baby in a particular way by their nursing methods. He had assembled a collection of x-rays, mostly brought from Vienna, during this study, but it no longer exists in the department.

Some members of the department, when interviewed many years later, reported that they believed Schüller was supported financially by John O'Sullivan, who was also attached to the Anatomy Department, and by Frank Morgan. It is strange that this story did not spread a kilometre to the east and become part of the folklore of the x-ray department in St Vincent's. This story might have been due to a misunderstanding on the part of the anatomists, but it made its way into the official history of the Anatomy School in the University of Melbourne from a highly reliable source.[5]

When the Schüllers arrived their financial situation was precarious, and it is entirely consistent with what is known of both these men that they may have supported the Schüllers, at least for a time.

No sooner had Schüller settled into the hospital than a plan which had been developed in the Victorian Division of the Royal Australasian College of Surgeons gave prospect of a widened career for the professor. This had been developed by two senior fellows of the college, Hugh Devine and Alan Newton. Devine was the president of the College at this time.

The idea was for the College, in conjunction with the University of Melbourne, or at least with university's blessing, to establish a postgraduate school of surgery in the newly reconstructed Prince Henry's Hospital. The two men had been quietly discussing this with Raymond Priestley, the Vice Chancellor of the University, and the Prince Henry's management for two or three years. Devine presented a prospectus to a meeting of the Executive Committee of the College (now the Council) on 18 December 1939 in which he presented their detailed recommendations, which included Arthur Schüller on the teaching faculty.

The Executive Committee comprised elected representatives from all the other state divisions; the numbers went against the President and the Victorian group. The move was quashed. It was all very well (or bad enough) to have the College headquarters in Melbourne but to have the postgraduate school there as well was going too far for the others.

We do not know now whether Schüller was aware of this plan, but since both Devine and Newton were well acquainted with Schüller's work, it is worth mentioning the connections. Alan Newton had bought a copy of the professor's magnum opus in the original German edition when it came out in 1912; Hugh Devine had taken the Vienna course in radiology in 1908. Newton had donated his copy of *Röntgen Diagnosis of Diseases of the Head* to the College library when it was set up years later.

In 1988, an unsympathetic and perhaps ill-informed librarian struggling with an overcrowded collection removed the book from the stacks and sent it to the second-hand booksellers. It was discovered there by Doctor Herbert Bower (Bauer), who rescued it. Bower, who had come from Vienna in 1938, spent the war in northern Australia working with defence construction gangs, but when he came to Melbourne he was forced to repeat the clinical years of the medical course before he could be licensed. For this he came to St Vincent's Hospital Clinical School in the late 1940s and went on to become a distinguished psychiatrist. He gave the book to the author in 2001; it is now included in the archive of Schüller's books and papers.

The Schüller story is riddled with coincidental linkages between individuals and across nations, an indication of the widespread interest evoked by his work and teaching, as well as being a reflection on his personal popularity.

From the beginning there was the possibility of difficulties in the relationship between Arthur Schüller and Frank Morgan. University professors in Vienna were accorded great respect and high social and academic status, and now Schüller, the internationally acknowledged master, found himself in a junior position to a man more than thirty years younger.

Further, he would have to contend with Morgan's formal expectations of hierarchical relationships. Between the pair of them, they solved any difficulties brilliantly. Appearances clearly indicated that the professor was part of the x-ray department; that was where he was lodged and there were no problems. Very quickly, partly because of mutual personal affinities and partly because of Schüller's specialist importance to neurosurgery, neurosurgery became Arthur's natural home.

Without doubt there was also an element of hero worship in

Morgan's appreciation of Schüller. In spite of what many young observers thought bordered on the obsequious, Schüller always stood his ground, defending his expertise and reputation with confidence in the event of any disparity of opinion, but Morgan was never bested.

Differences in opinion could only arise with Frank Morgan, and they seem to have been mercifully infrequent. Arthur Schüller had his own status to defend, but so did Frank Morgan; he was the anointed head of the hospital neurosurgical unit, and the first fully and formally trained neurosurgeon to be appointed as such to an Australian teaching hospital. The appointment dated from the middle of 1936, when he was still training in London with Hugh Cairns and he took it up in December of that year.

Before that time some neurosurgery was done at St Vincent's by general surgeons, notably by Leo Doyle, and there were others, senior in years to Morgan, in other places who were doing some neurosurgery in their own hospitals, while practicing general surgery, most of whom had not undergone any formal neurosurgical training elsewhere.

Arthur Schüller most certainly recognised Morgan's status as the head of the unit; Morgan certainly did. In his view, the opinion of the head of a clinic, any clinic, was never to be questioned; any implied suggestion to the contrary among the lower ranks was dealt with by stating his objection to a point with exquisite courtesy, declaring it to be in error and repeating this, briefly and kindly, the next day and the day after that and the day after that if he thought it necessary. This particularly applied to references to the fresh literature of the day by enthusiastic junior ranks; they ran the risk of being regarded as disrespectful.

In later years Frank Morgan related to even the most senior and experienced of his assistant surgeons along similar lines, in relation to matters of diagnosis, management and distribution of surgical responsibilities, and yet overt difficulties almost never arose. They recognised his determined insistence on the recognition of his chosen public and professional persona, which he did with extraordinary consistency over a lifetime, at all times and levels and, for the most part, it was an efficient and reasonably harmonious working arrangement.

There is one certain example of the application of the above corrective technique to Arthur Schüller and, if there were others, they must have been exceedingly rare. Schüller would have learned that lesson very quickly. The two men lived in a state of mutual respect and deepening affection for the rest of their lives together. Schüller recognised that a radiologist, no matter how knowledgeable, must always be at a disadvantage in discourse with an experienced neurosurgeon involving surgical treatment; he recognised that Frank Morgan was a product of the Cushing school of neurosurgery, which Schüller admired, as was Morgan's contemporary Joe Pennybacker, who had so impressed Schüller in Oxford; both were trained by Cairns in the mid-thirties at the London Hospital, a few years before Cairns moved to the Chair of Surgery in Oxford.

It was a wonderful friendship decorated with Schüller's Viennese courtesies and Morgan's carefully honed manners of the previous generation and beyond. Many, from those days, have recorded their edification and delight at observing these two men in mutually affectionate and respectful action with all the grace, not always without some amusement among the irreverent juniors. Morgan always emphasised Schüller's mastery and Schüller expressed his admiration for Morgan's surgery to everybody.

The seniority of Morgan's concept of status was reflected in his preference for moving among people older than himself; this was partly because he was chosen, at an early age, to serve on various important hospital committees. But, more important, was his own expectation of recognition and respect for seniority and authority. He was a man of unswerving loyalty to what he saw as constituted authority – Church, State, Hospital and individual people to whom he was committed; he expected a like recognition in his own case.

To some extent this attitude was inevitable; he was a young man appointed to a new senior position while his contemporaries occupied the lower ranks, and charged with the burden of establishing his specialty in the hospital and in the wider community against scepticism in some places. He had to prove that he and neurosurgery had something very special to offer, and he delivered the proof. In his own quiet way, Frank Morgan studiously attracted attention to whatever he was doing in those early years. He chose to embellish his style with some remarkably exaggerated attentions to detail, such as bringing patients from the wards to the operating room and covering them from head to foot with sterile drapes to perform a simple lumbar puncture; this certainly got the message across.

On one memorable occasion in Morgan's early days, a very senior and rather pompous general physician came into the operating room to inspect this young man at work, wearing only a gown over his street clothes, which was a breach of aseptic ritual. He loomed up behind the surgeon's shoulder and was promptly moved, with Morgan's usual exquisite tact and courtesy, indeed ceremony, to a safe distance from the exposed brain.

Professor Schüller was always known as such or "the Professor", although he never used the title himself, always announcing himself on the telephone as "*hier ist Doktor Schüller*". He moved freely between the x-ray department and the neurosurgical ward, soon forging lasting friendships with the nuns in charge of the two departments, and for the first ten years or so he was in the hospital at 7.30 am.

Initially this was something of a novelty since Frank Morgan, cast in the English mode of the 1930s, did not arrive before 9 am. Schüller's first move each morning was to visit any children, in a small annex just off the adult ward; not infrequently he had a small item of confectionery in the pocket of his coat which he slipped to them when the eyes of the ward authorities were elsewhere. The professor then went to the adult beds and began taking histories and making neurologic examinations, recording them in the patient's notes. If junior residents or registrars were about the ward, he demonstrated his findings and gave them a short tutorial.

The next move was to the x-ray department or the operating room. This was the pattern of his days until the late 1940s. Schüller attended ward rounds and weekly outpatient clinics as well as the operating sessions, where he would assist Frank Morgan. He was always careful never to disrobe in the surgeons change room when others were present, which meant that he arrived in the operating room a little later than the rest of the team. This was attributed by some observers to his sensitivity about the x-ray burns on his thighs and lower legs, and was confirmed in conversation with the author, in whom he had enough confidence to also mention his radiation-induced infertility.

The professor would often offer a running comment of questions, observations and even advice during time in the operating room and wards. Morgan often found these burdensome, and sometimes the enthusiast was quietly muffled into silence. This assistant role was not a daily event but mostly confined to intracranial procedures, spinal cord tumours and the newly emerging surgery for lumbar disc prolapse, particularly if the x-ray pictures interested him. He always found inspection of the living pathology a source of pleasure.

Visits to the pathology department to inspect neurosurgical biopsy specimens and attendance at the daily hospital post-mortem examinations brought Schüller into early contact with Andrew Brenan, head of the department, resulting in a close friendship between the two.

Like O'Sullivan, he was a regular attendant at the midday post-mortem examinations on cases of interest. In 1940 Brenan decided that a photographic portrait of Arthur was required and he undertook the necessary arrangements. The chosen photographer was Julian Smith, a former senior surgeon in the hospital who had retired in the mid-1930s. Smith was no "mere" amateur; his work was widely known nationally and internationally; he had exhibited in Paris and London and was an elected member of the Royal Society of Photographers.

Julian Smith was familiar with the sight of the professor on his visits to the hospital and had noted the large shock of white hair, which reminded him of Albert Einstein. He secretly decided that he would cast Schüller in that mould. The day after the event, the angry and disappointed Julian Smith, noted for his volatile temperament, burst through Andrew Brenan's door and shouted, "The idiot went and had his hair cut!" It was a fortunate disaster, for it produced one of Julian Smith's masterpieces, and certainly the best photograph ever discovered of Arthur Schüller.[6]

Frank Morgan never entered his ward without the registrar, who walked at his side. Arthur Schüller invariably took up a secondary position behind them. In all his years at the hospital, he did not wear a white coat, which was standard for all medical personnel, paramedics (as we would call them today), laboratory scientists and other professionals. His uniform was a grey dust coat of the sort worn then by men in tool stores and hardware shops; but it was not abandoned after he received registration as a medical practitioner in 1946. The reason for this extraordinary attire was never divulged to the junior staff and Morgan never referred to it, but it struck all observers as inexcusably demeaning.

This may reflect the fact that Schüller, for reasons stated above, appears never to have been formally appointed to the medical staff. It seems possible that Schüller made that decision himself, preferring to maintain a modest profile when even the radiographers wore white coats.

At times the professor's refined Viennese manners of the imperial age seemed to border on the subservient, which horrified many of the witnesses who now provide their reminiscences. It should be remembered that these witnesses, in the mid-1940s and later, were young people in their early and middle twenties for the most part. Many of these had passed on by the time when the reminiscences were garnered, beginning about the year 2000, and since Arthur Schüller left the hospital in 1956 and died the following year, reliable witnesses were few. Some of their perceptions and judgments may well have been less emotional in their mature years.

Some young observers judged Morgan harshly for his serene

assumption of superiority in the presence of the great professor. Others were impressed by the professor's hesitancy and apparent timidity. Lacking experience of the wider world, they did not understand the full implications for a man of magisterial world authority who had lost his homeland, his international audience for postgraduate teaching sessions, his prestigious university title, which was socially so important in Vienna, and who now suffered a sense of dependency on the hospital and its people. Doubtless they did not realise that Morgan had status to defend or at least to define in those early years of his career, nor did they appreciate his need for unruffled authority.

Throughout 1944 Arthur Schüller's position in the long x-ray reporting room among the other radiologists must have been at times uncomfortable and embarrassing. The two senior radiologists, John O'Sullivan and Leo King, had differences of opinion which became obvious to the others.

Fortunately, 1945 would bring a satisfactory resolution of this.

St Vincent's Hospital Melbourne in the 1940s. The front entrance can be seen to the right of the elm tree in the foreground. The X Ray Department was in the basement of this building. During his last admission to hospital, Schüller was in a ward on the second floor in a bed that looked over Victoria Parade, the large street in the foreground of this picture.

This picture of the Schüllers was taken in 1942 by a street photographer in Collins Street, Melbourne. Grete in particular would have been regarded as a very well-dressed for the times.

The "Professor" at work, St Vincent's Hospital Melbourne. The photograph dates from the early 1940s and was almost certainly taken by Pat Sullivan, the Chief Radiographer, also an excellent amateur photographer and friend of Arthur.

The Professor at work in his office in the Department of Radiology at St Vincent's Hospital. Characteristically, the door is open and Schüller is wearing his grey laboratory coat. On the desk can be seen the school exercise book in which he wrote his short reports for typing at the end of the day.

Chapter Seven

1945

Still
The world out-Herods Herod; and the year,
The nineteen hundred forty-fifth of grace
Lumbers with losses up the clinkered hill
Of our purgation.

"The Holy Innocents"
– Robert Lowell

Nineteen forty-five was to be a turning point in the Schüllers' lives; it brought forth a multitude of events, some worthy of celebration, some consoling, others unutterably tragic.

John O'Sullivan stepped down from his directorship of the combined sections of diagnostic and therapeutic radiology, and moved down to the other end of the long subterranean corridor of the x-ray department to devote his time entirely to radiotherapy. He took Arthur Schüller with him and installed him in an office of his own. This recognised Schüller's stature and gave him, incidentally, the privacy and quietude which he would need for his grieving to come, but it separated him from the companionable distractions of the other radiologists. The move both reflected the tensions between O'Sullivan and the other senior radiologist, Leo King, which had precipitated the split, and demonstrated O'Sullivan's understandable proprietary concern for Schüller's interests.

The war had ground on with all its anxieties and uncertainties for the Schüllers, but as time went on, it was evident that Germany would lose the war and truths would emerge. Rumours were plentiful along the refugee grapevine, and from official sources, but no reliable information had reached the Schüllers about their sons, daughter-in-law and granddaughter, or about Grete's mother, Frederike Stiassni. Grete spoke often about the boys to her friends, but Arthur endured in silence. Hope must have been fading from late 1944 onwards as the trickle of fact and rumour about the murderous German atrocities mounted.

On the 15 April 1945 the British 11th Armoured Division entered Belsen to find scenes of indescribable horror. Almost immediately the news of this broke all over the world, followed quickly by newsreels in the cinemas. Arthur Schüller must have heard some of the radio news at the very least, but he went on with the work, examining his x-ray films and writing his reports in the usual manner, giving friendly welcomes to people coming to him with questions.

On 7 May, the Allies reached the top of Robert Lowell's purgatorial hill and the war against Germany ended. There was no suggestion that Schüller's sons were in Belsen, but now he knew what he must confront in the coming months. There was no escape from this; throughout 1945 newspaper and cinema newsreel accounts of the numerous other labour and extermination camps seemed neverending.

On 16 May, Schüller gave an invited guest lecture to the Society of Australasian Neurological Surgeons, which was later to change its name to the Neurosurgical Society of Australasia (NSA), on the history of cordotomy, a re-run of the lecture he gave to the Medical Students Society at the university in 1942. He carried it off without showing evidence of his distress. In the group photograph after the meeting he was again placed at the centre of the front row as he had been in Antwerp on his last day in Continental Europe.

It is surprising that he was not nominated for honorary membership, because Frank Morgan was the honorary secretary at the time, and his friend and colleague. Douglas Miller in Sydney would have readily seconded the motion. Perhaps the very young society had not evolved to that point; the Neurosurgical Society had held its inaugural meeting in 1940 and it did not meet again until 1945. The minutes of this meeting, written by Frank Morgan, are lodged in the archives at the Royal Australasian College of Surgeons; there is no mention of any business meeting.

Schüller must have felt, to some extent, the consolation of being at home on this occasion; the first part of the meeting was held at St Vincent's Hospital where he was certainly on home ground, and at the invitation of Professor Sidney Sunderland, the second part, in the afternoon, was held in the Anatomy School at the University of Melbourne.

In their early months in Australia, the Schüllers were still casting around for alternatives and, for a reason which cannot now be discovered, they lodged their German "passports", now valueless, with the Swiss Consulate in Melbourne (the Consulate holds no record of this).

In September 1944, the Schüllers had just completed residence in Australia for five years and their thoughts had turned to citizenship in postwar Australia. Arthur engaged a lawyer to sort out the paperwork. The testimony of two referees familiar with the applicant was required and he chose people whom he thought to be well-known outside the hospital.

John O'Sullivan, in whose department he worked, was an adviser to the Commonwealth Government Health Department on matters to do with radiology and radiotherapy, and Dr Kevin O'Day, the hospital's senior ophthalmologist, was nationally and internationally recognised for his researches and publications on the comparative anatomy of the eye. O'Day operated a personal histology laboratory in the pathology department, sharing his facilities with the neurosurgical unit for the processing of biopsy and post-mortem specimens which sometimes required special techniques; Arthur was a frequent visitor.

On 19 May 1945, he received his Certificate of Naturalisation as an Australian citizen and the "refugee alien" status was cancelled; along with this, his wife automatically became an Australian citizen. The validating act involved handing in his refugee alien's registration card at the local police station and swearing allegiance to His Majesty the King.

John O'Sullivan, probably mindful of the objections raised to Schüller's election as an honorary member of The Australian and New Zealand Association of Radiologists in 1941, appears to have decided to lie low for the time being. His colleagues naturally expected that now the time had come for Schüller to apply for registration as a medical practitioner, but again the process stalled. Presumably the Victorian government, preoccupied with all the problems of demobilisation of the military and the financial chaos with which wars end, had little interest in fixing the problems of the Medical Board and eventually the remedy, the *Medical Practitioner Registration Act* 1946 came into law the following year.

In the meantime, Schüller continued in his restricted private practice in Collins Street, relying upon the annual renewal of the licence to practise that was conferred originally by the Commonwealth Alien Doctors Board in 1942. The final extension was granted in January 1946, and it was his last encounter with that bureaucracy.

The final process of his registration under Victorian law, which gave him full practising rights, did not occur until December 1946 but, as will be told, at least part of this process was hardly a bureaucratic encounter.

On 1 July, the University of Melbourne formally recognised his appointment as Honorary Research Fellow which Sidney Sunderland had made in 1942. Morgan later reported that Arthur Schüller was particularly pleased with this; he set great value on academic attachment. With the confidence of his new citizenship in hand, Schüller did not proceed through Sunderland and wait to be invited. He took the Vienna path and applied for it directly in writing to the University Council. Melbourne University appointed Schüller for an indefinite period, which expired only with his death.

In November 1945, Schüller's friend Walter Dandy at Johns Hopkins sent him a copy of his book on Intracranial Aneurysms, on the frontispiece of which he had written: "You are the greatest roentgenologist of all time". Schüller and Dandy had forged a friendship since their first meeting in the early 1920s. There are no preserved letters to or from Schüller in the Johns Hopkins archives, until the last year in Vienna, which gave rise to the preserved correspondence noted in the chapter on the Anschluss. Nevertheless, Dandy sent Schüller copies of all his books from that time on.

It appears that Schüller began writing to friends in Vienna in the last half of 1945 but, characteristically, the correspondence he received was never preserved except for one short communication which was clearly stored accidentally between the leaves of one of Arthur's own books as a bookmark; it was discovered only a few years ago. This came from Dr Georgina Holzknecht, herself a radiologist, and sister of his friend and colleague Guido Holzknecht. It was in reply to a number of questions which he had put to her. She told him that Hans Hoff was returning from America to become the Director of the Institute of Neurology but E. G. Mayer remained there because he could not secure a guarantee that he would become the Director of the Institute of Radiology, a position which he had been about to assume before Heinrich Himmler and Eduard Pernkopf intervened.

Schüller's correspondence was soon spread more widely; he was in contact with B. G. Ziedses des Plantes, the Dutch genius of radiographic imaging around this time.

In the last half of the 1940s, the folklore of the x-ray department at St Vincent's had it that Schüller had written to the editor of the American surgical journal *Surgery* suggesting that he run a birthday issue for Walter Dandy in the early part of 1946. The official biography of Dandy commissioned by the Congress of Neurological Surgeons records that the suggestion came from "Australian friends". Nevertheless, it is almost certain that Schüller and Frank Morgan were at least in part responsible for it. Arthur Schüller followed this up by submitting a paper on cephalohaematoma deformans in the hope that it would appear in the birthday issue, but it was not published until after Dandy's sudden and premature death on 19 April 1946, just two weeks after his sixtieth birthday.

And then in December came the report on the events which had engulfed the Schüllers' sons in the time since Arthur had last seen them in April 1939. As the German Army retreated from the East, Brno was overrun by the Russians, and it was a long time before anyone else gained access.

Lieutenant Charles Stiassni, son of Ernst Stiassni, nephew of Grete Schüller and cousin of the Schüller boys, believed he was the first American officer to be allowed to enter the city. Doubtless he was chosen by his superiors because he had lived his early years there before the war, leaving Czechoslovakia for America in 1938. After graduating from Columbia University, to which he had been admitted shortly after his arrival, he had joined the US Army and served in the Italian campaign, before being seconded to the intelligence service (OSS) and the Army Committee for the Investigation of War Crimes. He was sent down from Prague to investigate the fates of the people of Brno and he was able to interview a number of survivors of Auschwitz and Theresienstadt and friends of the Stiassni and Schüller families.

On 8 October 1945, Lt Stiassni wrote his report in true professional intelligence officer style and presented it in the form of a letter to his parents with a request to pass on a copy to the Schüllers. It is a remarkable document, and was in the possession of one of Grete's nieces, all the more remarkable and moving for the detached objectivity of the writer, standing at a distance from its contents. The stories are told in precise lucid prose, the details without qualification and with minimal comment. There is no expression of sadness, no cry of anguish or outrage, nothing to distract the reader from the bare facts.

If Schüller revealed his anguish to Morgan, as seems likely, it went no further, but within the hospital community he said nothing and his work continued without interruption. He played his violin in the resident doctors' concert that year but he never appeared again.

This picture of Sister Mary Cephas was probably taken in the late 1940s. Sister Cephas was the nun in charge of the Radiology Department at St Vincent's Hospital, Melbourne, in the 1940s and 50s. She became a great friend of Arthur Schüller. Whilst the fern garden may look contrived, Sister Mary was a very keen gardener and set up an exotic plantation in a secluded area outside the Radiology Department.

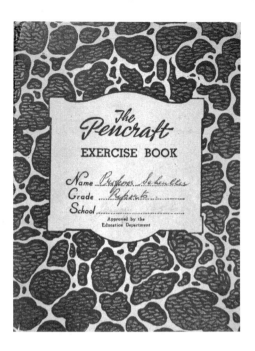

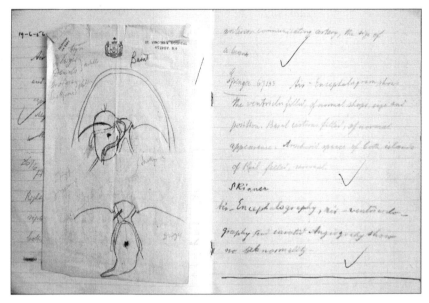

Schüller usually wrote his reports in a school exercise book. This picture is from the last of these books dated January 1956. The reports were characteristically short. At the end of the day the book was handed over to the typists. The typed report was reviewed and signed off by Schüller the next day. The open exercise book is on a typical page and includes a piece of hospital notepaper found in the book with details of cases he had been reporting.

This photograph is of the participants of the Second Meeting of the Australasian Neurological Surgeons on the morning of Wednesday, 16 May 1945 in front of the old anatomy building at the University of Melbourne. The afternoon session was held at St Vincent's Hospital. Schüller is in the front row left centre and a young Frank Morgan is immediately behind him to the left.

Two formal photographs of Schüller taken in the late 1940s by Pat Sullivan, the chief radiographer at St Vincent's Hospital.

The famous portrait of Arthur Schüller taken in the 1940s by Julian Smith, the eccentric but extraordinarily talented photographer and surgeon. Smith was furious when Schüller arrived for the photograph having had a haircut the day before. Schüller at that time had a fine crop of hair and Smith hoped to capture his exuberant mane in a similar fashion to the celebrated photograph of Albert Einstein. In the end both Smith and Schüller were delighted with the result (this was the photograph in my father's study).

Chapter Eight

In Illo Tempore

Dead children
Were trying to reach you – Oh gently, gently
Show him an honest, confident task done – guide him
Close to the garden, give him preponderance
Over those nights –

"The Third Duino Elegy"
– Rainer Maria Rilke
Translated by J B Leishman & Stephen Spender

They have only gone for a walk
Up to the mountains.
They have only gone out ahead of us
And do not want to come home again.
We will find them on those heights up there
In the sunshine.

Kindertotenlieder (Songs on the Death of Children)
– words by Friedrich Rückert
– songs by Gustav Mahler

"The following is an account of the last years of Grandmamma Stiassni and the Schüller boys." – Lt Charles Stiassni, US Army. October 8th 1945.

The letter was addressed to his parents with instructions to forward to others, including his uncle, Arthur Schüller. Charles was at least ten years younger than his two cousins Franz and Hans, whom he had known in Brno before the war.[7]

There followed a listing of people and events, heartbreaking even to an outsider almost seventy-five years later. In a sense, it is more than a letter to a family; it is a report to the world and it demands that some of it be told here, embedded in what history tells us of the time.

❧

Hitler's preoccupation with the appearances of legality determined a particular situation in the ironically named Protectorates of Bohemia and Moravia, which were what was left of Czechoslovakia after Slovakia had been separated. These were not quite the same as other conquered territories, or so Hitler would have the world believe. The local authorities were allowed some slack and the first Protector, Constantin von Neurath, rewarded for his earlier work on the Sudeten question, was a moderate.

At first the application of the Nuremberg Laws and the restriction of Jewish liberties were less stringent than elsewhere; in time that was to change with dreadful ferocity, particularly after the assassination in Prague of Reinhard Heydrich, who succeeded von Neurath as Protector of Moravia.

It is now certain that the Schüller boys, Franz and Hans, were both in Brno, for whatever reasons, when the "Protecting" army moved in. At one time Franz and his family had a visa for Yugoslavia, but his wife broke a leg while skiing in Slovakia and they were trapped by the German progress before she was ready to move. The neighbouring countries closed their borders and their entrance visas were withdrawn.

Initially the boys were left in their own homes and their grandmother, the eighty-four-year-old Frederike Stiassni, known to those close to her as Riki, remained in her house at Hroznova 7. Poldi Pokorna, her non-Jewish servant and full-time companion, continued to live in, and another non-Jewish servant, Marie Nimmerfrohova,

132

who came in by day, moved in with them in August 1939. The bridge parties with Jewish and non-Jewish friends continued and there were many visits from others. Frederike took daily walks, but not in the woods, which were for non-Jewish people only.

Later in 1939 an official of the *Devisenschutzkommando* (foreign exchange authority) came from Vienna to confiscate the Stiassni textile factory, but the German authorities mistakenly believed that Grete's brother Rudolf, a long-time resident of Switzerland, was a Swiss citizen, and the plant was not completely appropriated at first. After this Frederike was harassed periodically by financial control officers, billeting officers and the Gestapo, who made threatening visits to the house. At these times, Poldi hid her in a small room and dealt with them herself.

In the spring of 1940 Frederike's bank account was frozen and she was given a small one-off payment which did not last long. Small cash payments, brought by a functionary of the factory, dwindled, and soon this woman could bring no more. Thereafter some non-Jewish friends, Mr and Mrs Hödl, brought money regularly for food.

Before this, Mrs Hödl had made regular clandestine visits through the back garden of a neighbour, but later this became impossible without risk of arrest. Then Poldi made regular trips to the Hödls' home to report and receive further financial support.

At about this time the boys were taken for forced labour – Franz to Prague to work in a laundry, Hans to break stones in a nearby rock quarry at Jundrof. They did not meet again until Hans was deported to Theresienstadt, where Franz had been sent before him.

At Christmas 1940 a family party was organised by the servant women; Hans and his wife Gerda were present.[8] Just months later, the situation deteriorated. It became forbidden for non-Jewish people to be employed by Jewish people, or even to associate with them. The wearing of the yellow star on the street was now rigorously enforced and Poldi could no longer be seen out of doors with Frederike.

In March 1941, Frederike was evicted from her home and "concentrated" in a single room in another Jewish household. Poldi, nominally employed by a woman from the Stiassni company to shield her from the scrutiny of the Gestapo, secretly moved in with her, in defiance of the regulations. Their walks were confined to the small garden where Gerda brought Frederike's "newborn" [sic] great-granddaughter Eva to see her.[9]

A month later Hans and his family were confined to a single room above a jeweller's shop, and in September Frederike was moved again to a half-room with a thin wooden partition. She became ill and was nursed by Poldi and Marie in twenty-four-hour shifts. There were no cooking facilities; Marie brought in all meals except on Sundays when Hans, who was still able to visit her, brought the dinner.

> Marie describes how Christmas 1941 was celebrated there in the Bratislavska; she had a great meal with fish etc. and the four, including Mrs Hönig from the other side of the partition, Grandmama, Poldi and Marie had a very gay time. They only went home after 11.

February saw another forced move to a shared single room. Hans, caught smuggling coal to them, was sent to the Kounicovy Koleje, a student accommodation house in Brno that had become a notorious Gestapo prison.

For some time there had been a steady flow of deportations and at the end of March the SS decided on a local "final solution". All remaining Jews in Brno were ordered to report at the Sennenfeld School, on foot and carrying their own baggage, on 14 April 1942. On the last night many friends visited, and Marie and Poldi remained with Frederike all night: "Into her clothes these two loyal servants sewed many thousands of crowns."

Too old to walk the distance, too frail to carry her burden, her friends forbidden to help, Frederike Stiassni was taken by the SS at 6 am and dumped on the floor of a horse-drawn furniture van. Mr and Mrs Hödl, in defiance of the Gestapo, saw off this miserable tumbril. After three days at the school and two on a train, shunted around on Eichmann's railway system, presumably tightly packed in cattle trucks to judge from already established SS practice, half-blind and over eighty years old, she must have arrived at the Theresienstadt "model ghetto", exhausted and ill.

Gerda and Eva were transported around the same time; the mother and child were separated on the train but came together again in the camp. Franz already had been sent from Prague, and Hans, released from prison for another end, came shortly after.[10]

Theresienstadt (now Terezín in the Czech Republic), about sixty kilometres from Prague, was originally planned as a special ghetto formed by the simple expedient of relocating its inhabitants and sealing the entire town. Built originally by the Habsburg Emperor Joseph II as a garrison town to control the Empire's subject peoples, and named for his mother the Empress Maria Therese, it had lost its military function by the late nineteenth century.

The initial plan was to accommodate the privileged Jews, mainly from Austria and Czechoslovakia, living in "comparative comfort" to the end of their days. Its public face aimed at the illusion of a benign centre; it was not to be a killing site and there were no gas chambers. "Privilege" was defined by age, distinction in music, arts and sciences, former high military rank, loyal military service, academic status, erstwhile wealth and influence, and connections with the famous. It was even to have a coffee shop.

The scheme was not maintained for long. German conquests in the east brought more Jewish people into German territory, deportations to Theresienstadt were stepped up, food rations were cut back, overcrowding became critical – at times there were sixty thousand in a town meant for six thousand – and, inevitably, the SS guards became progressively brutalised. The mortality rate was tragically high from starvation and medical neglect, repeated beatings, random acts of unutterable brutality and sporadic summary executions, as was the case in other ghettos and camps. The model ghetto slid down the slope of depravity and became in turn a concentration camp, a forced labour exchange and a centre for that macabre process of triage, the "selections" for deportation to the extermination camps. It ended in shuttle trains between Theresienstadt and Auschwitz-Birkenau.

Age, either very young or very old, was no safeguard against "selection" for Auschwitz and other places. The sisters of Sigmund Freud, both in their eighties, were killed, as was a sister of Ludwig Wittgenstein. In fact, the elderly, the broken, the starved, the sick and the children were officially nominated for priority in selection for Auschwitz-Birkenau because they were useless for labour and a drain on resources. Many of these people were marched straight from the train to the gas chambers.

By dying in Theresienstadt, Frederike Stiassni cheated the system in a sense; she died on 19 April 1942, lying on some straw on the floor of a derelict old building, five days after she was removed from Brno. She was unconscious when Hans saw her at the end.

Mail was permitted in and out of the ghetto in its early days, and Poldi sent food parcels to Hans, some of which got past the guards. Posting the articles involved some risk, so she went to the mailbox at night. The situation changed as Theresienstadt moved along its tragic spectrum of functions.

The postal service was stopped in November 1943, after which she heard no more of Hans. The Gestapo continued their interest in Poldi; in fear for her life, she destroyed his letters with the exception of the small black-edged card on which he announced the death of Frederike Stiassni:

> Liebe Poldi,
> Riki died peacefully on 19 April.
> Pneumonia and pleurisy. Inform
> Anna. – Evi has a cold.
> Hans

Poldi Pokorna offered the card to Charles Stiassni but he could not take it from her.

Liebe Poldi indeed.

⁂

Franz remained in Prague, working as slave labour in a laundry until 20 November 1942, when he was sent to Theresienstadt and then on to Auschwitz, which he reached on 23 January 1943.[11]

Auschwitz had been constructed as a border fortress against the eastern Slavs in the early years of the Habsburg lineage. It was the Ostmark, the Eastern March of the Germanic States, the eastern limit of the Empire at that time. After the Anschluss, the Germans used Ostmark as a term for Vienna, the eastern limit of the new Germany.

Among the titles of Franz Josef, the protector of Arthur Schüller and his generation, was Duke of Auschwitz. Himmler, who ordered the construction of both Auschwitz and Theresienstadt, must have known of their historical significance.

Along with Franz went six thousand others on that train, of whom only two hundred and fifty remained alive at the end of that year. There was no trace of him when Hans arrived on 15 December 1943; surviving friends reported that he had disappeared within a few weeks.

Hans and Gerda, who were transferred at about the same time, were spared at first, for there was much to be done in extending the buildings, in the sand and gravel pits, and operating and extending the synthetic rubber factory operated by IG Farben, knowingly built in the Birkenau camp.

Gerda and Eva disappeared within a few weeks of Hans' departure from Auschwitz in June or July 1944, down the stairs to those subterranean rooms so reassuringly marked as sauna, change rooms, delousing, and then the showers from which there was no return.

In June 1944, Hans was caught smuggling cigarettes into the camp (for trading) and sentenced to three months in the *Straf Kompanie* (punishment unit) – which few survived – only to be returned after three days. Within a few weeks Hans was tranferred to another camp, probably Buchenwald, presumably to cover a shortage of workers.[12]

Nothing further was heard of Hans.

Eva was five years old.

The Stiassni family in the late 1920s. Grete's mother, Frederike is centre and Grete is to her right. Arthur Schüller stands immediately behind his mother-in-law. The two young men in the back row on the left are the two Schüller sons, Hans and Franz standing next to their maternal uncle Ernst Stiassni. Next to him is Alfred Stiasni standing next to Arthur. The older Stiassni brother Rudolf is probably second from the right, back row. The location is not identifiable but is probably not the Schüller residence in Vienna, possibly Brno, given that all the Stiassni family was present. If so, it is possibly Alfred Stiassni's architecturally stunning residence he built in Brno in the late twenties (Vila Stiassni, now a Czech National Heritage site).

Prague, October 8, 1945.

Letter No 71, page1.

Dear Parents: (cc to Joe, Alfred, Arthur Schüller, Herrmann) *Rudolf*

    The following is an account of the last years of Grandmama Stiassni and the Schüller boys. The information is based on statements by Poldi Pokorna who was grandmama's constant companion in Brno until her departure to Terezin, Marie Nimmerfrohova, who substantiated Poldi's information. Further information on the life in the various concentration camps was presented by Miss Terese Haas, who was in Terezin during grandmama's only fourteen days there, and by Konrad Tutsch, who was to-gether with Hans and his family until July 1944.

    On the evening of March 14, 1939 grandmama was together was Hans and Gerda, who had just returned from a skiing trip in Slovakia, where Hans had broken his foot. That night Grete Knonorsa and Mr. Kulik, Alfred's chaufeur, came to take grandmama in a car to Austria and Switzerland. Poldi had prepared everything already, however the party was forced to turn back when they reached Jihlava, because the German troops would not let them pass.

The head of the letter dated 8 October 1945, Prague, by Lt Charles Stiassni (US Army) to his parents about the fate of Grandmother Stiassni, the Schüller boys, as well as Hans' wife and child, with instructions to pass it on to other members of the family, including Arthur Schüller.

Chapter Nine

Winding Down

From 1946, Schüller became a sad quiet man and was probably overtaken by clinical depression as time went on. An ominous sign was the appearance on his bookshelf of a monograph on frontal lobotomy for mental illness by the Americans Freeman and Watts, one of them a neurosurgeon and the other a psychiatrist. In those days, these procedures were at an early stage of development and were unacceptably and crudely destructive. For the most part, they were used only in the treatment of the violently disturbed. Ultimately Schüller asked Frank Morgan to undertake this procedure for him, but Morgan wisely believed that it would ruin a fine mind and he managed to dissuade the professor.

Schüller sat all day at his desk, a pile of x-rays in front of him. The desk was positioned against a wall on which was mounted a viewing box. He sat directly opposite the door, which was always open, his profile in full view of everyone passing along the corridor. Mostly he sat in silence, pondering the films in front of him and often with a skull on the bench at his left hand. His reports were written with a pencil in a schoolchild's exercise book which was returned from time to time to the typing pool in the office. Almost everybody knew about the great professor in the basement, and he was constantly the momentary centre of attention of all passers-by. Few of them paused to wave or say a friendly word, not because of antipathy or indifference but because most of them were young people, nurses and junior doctors, who were in awe of him and reluctant to impose themselves on the great man. Nevertheless they were always welcome and greeted with a short cry of pleasure. A casual conversation did not last long.

He was at once the most exposed and enclosed person in the hospital.

For most of the day he sat in silent contemplation of the films or studying a book, an almost monastic figure. Seen from the corridor, framed in the doorway, his profile was remarkably reminiscent of his personal bookplate, which depicts a monk in medieval garb, cowl turned back over the shoulders, contemplating a skull held in the right hand.

Apart from the passing parade in the corridor outside, he could look up to his right at the junction between wall and ceiling where there was a line of glass bricks on a level with the footpath, through which he could see the vague images of feet passing on the street.

He went to the other end of the corridor, where the general radiologists were about their business, less frequently as time went by; they were always busy and with little time to spend in conversation. This problem arose from their function as unpaid visiting specialists, which was the model for the university teaching hospitals in those days; they had their own private affairs to attend to as soon as their commitments to the hospital were fulfilled.

He moved about the corridors between the x-ray department, the neurosurgical ward and the emergency or casualty department, where he was a familiar figure. A film displaying a skull fracture was immediately personally delivered to the junior doctors in emergency and explained to them. He rarely visited the wards other than the neurosurgical, where he was part of the unit.

His freedom of movement between the x-ray department and the neurosurgical ward gave rise to much amusement when contrasted with the relationship between the nun in charge of the ward and the nun in charge of the x-ray department, with both of whom the professor soon forged warm friendships. These were very senior commanders, with strong personalities and intense justifiable pride in their territories. One did not enter the territory of the other without a telephonic application for a visitor's pass, after which a cordial reception was guaranteed. At times the professor functioned as a clandestine courier for one or the other.

His natural shyness and his sense of "otherness" made him reluctant to enter other ward territory where he might not be known. Always at home in the neurosurgical ward, he also developed a friendship with the senior trained nurse working under the nun in charge.[13]

Originally Schüller took pleasure in teaching at all levels, but in the late 1940s and beyond, his response to a registrar seeking information was short and tended to fade off into a lack of interest. Sadly, he showed little interest in four young Austrians who had been brought to Australia by their parents immediately before the Second World War and who were now students in the St Vincent's Hospital Clinical School. When their presence was made known to him, he made no attempt to look them up.

By 1948, aged 74, he no longer attended ward rounds and operating sessions. At about this time a young neurologist (Dr John Billings) was appointed to the Morgan Neurosurgical Outpatients Clinic, at which time the professor withdrew from the clinic.

Gradually he withdrew from most of the other contacts, particularly from 1950 onwards as his depression deepened, and he ceased to drop in on the other radiologists at the mid-morning tea break. He then became better known to the radiographers than the radiologists, because he supervised the projections and exposures of all the films taken during encephalograms and ventriculograms.

There developed a strong friendship between Schüller and the senior radiographer in the radiotherapy department, Patrick Sullivan, whose office was in the next room. Sullivan was an expert amateur who functioned as the part-time hospital photographer; he took many photographs of "the Professor" over a period of almost twenty years. If Schüller required some small service, Sullivan delivered it. They shared a common immigrant status, Pat Sullivan having migrated from Ireland. He was a highly intelligent and well-read man who might have done other and higher things, had he been given the opportunities.

Fortunately, neurosurgery and ophthalmology shared the same technician for the preparation of biopsy specimens, which led Arthur Schüller into contact with Dr Kevin O'Day. The laboratory was in the pathology department, where Schüller formed a friendship with a junior pathologist, Leo Rowan, who was also on the staff of the academic Department of Pathology in the university a mile or so away. Rowan moved regularly between the two places, and was a willing courier delivering and returning books requested by the professor from the medical library. In those days the formal courier service between the university medical library and the hospital libraries was not well developed.

As Arthur Schüller approached the last decade of life and his career in St Vincent's Hospital, there were fortunately a few good experiences in the time left for him. The regulations governing the functions of the Medical Board of Victoria were changed by act of Parliament in 1946, and he applied for registration as a medical practitioner. The law required the applicant to present himself to the chairman of the medical board and an expert panel to answer questions bearing on his competence, potentially a time of embarrassment for both the applicant and the board members. He was invited by the chairman to take a seat and offered a cup of coffee, which he accepted. There followed a rather uncomfortable period of trivial conversation, after which the chairman congratulated Professor Schüller on his registration.

Schüller asked about the questions and the chairman replied that he had already delivered a satisfactory answer when he accepted the coffee. On his return to department, there was much merriment among his colleagues.

Schüller was now free to practise without restriction and he immediately set about admitting the occasional private patient to hospital for investigation under his care. He chose the Sacred Heart Hospital in the northern suburb of Moreland, a private hospital conducted by sisters of the German province of the Missionaries of the Sacred Heart order (MSC). It meant a taxi trip of about five miles each way from his base but it was an excellent choice. He continued his habitual low profile by performing air encephalograms on a Saturday or Sunday afternoon, assisted by the neurosurgical registrar from St Vincent's, who accompanied him, the department being opened specially. Most of these patients were children or young adults with severe chronic epilepsy and varying degrees of mental and physical handicap. The registrar administered a general anesthetic and Schüller then made a lumbar puncture, with the patient in the lateral position, and manipulated the air into the ventricular system to suit his particular purpose, all without a special skull table.

The author recalls, with a blend of sadness and delight, one such occasion as he, the registrar, and Schüller took a taxi from St Vincent's Hospital with the professor in a happy and talkative mood. Noting some confetti on the floor of the car, he questioned the driver about what he called a symptom of a wedding.

The pair were met at the door of the x-ray department by two excited and smiling German nuns; one of them was the head radiographer and the other in charge of a ward upstairs (Sr Egrnew Egr, originally from Westphalia and Sr Ethelredis Schutz, originally from Gdansk). Both of them were fluent in English, but the affairs of the afternoon were conducted entirely in German, of which the registrar (the author) understood not a word. It was a moving experience to note the happy chatter among this little group of "exiles" from their homelands so enjoying the meeting. They would never see their homes or families again. The afternoon concluded with a formal bow and kissing of the nuns' hands as he thanked and farewelled them.

Back in the hospital, Schüller forced a payment for services on the unwilling registrar who was not, in any case, permitted to work outside the hospital. On the following Monday, the professor came to the enquiry desk in the front hall of the hospital bearing a bag of fruit in gratitude for the calling of the taxi the day before. The recipient had not been on duty on the day in question, but that went unnoticed.

On 27 November 1947 the Australian government introduced laws to nationalise the banks. The banks immediately manned the barricades, taking the government to a number of legal challenges over the next two years; citizen Arthur Schüller joined their ranks. He had been ruined financially by the collapse of the Austrian economy in 1919 when the Austrian banking system had collapsed. Schüller was appalled at the prospect of another disaster and he wrote a personal letter to the Prime Minister of the Labor government, Ben Chifley, warning him of the consequences and, according to the folklore in the x-ray department, taking a decidedly admonitory tone which delighted his conservative colleagues.

Chifley sent a courteous reply over his personal signature. This also evoked a round of applause from the conservatives. After moving up the legal scale with a series of judgments and appeals, the case ended in the Privy Council in London which eventually decided, in June 1949, that nationalisation of the banks would be contrary to the Australian Constitution. Schüller enjoyed another day of fame.

In June 1947, he was unanimously elected to honorary membership of the Neurosurgical Society of Australasia at its meeting. There is something vaguely puzzling about this process; it was proposed by Frank Morgan, which is what would be expected, but it was seconded by the same Sydney neurosurgeon who had been at the centre of the difficulty concerning payment a year or so before. Perhaps this was a happy outcome from an embarrassing business.

In 1948, Professor Sir Hugh Cairns, the Nuffield Professor of Surgery in the University of Oxford, visited New Zealand and

Australia as the first Sims Travelling Professor on medical ambassadorial duties, giving lectures to the profession, taking student teaching sessions, and visiting hospitals. He came to St Vincent's Hospital and visited Schüller in his office, but this fell rather flat; Cairns had students to teach, there was more work to do on an important lecture to the general medical profession at Melbourne University that evening, and he wished to attend the theatre to watch Frank Morgan draining a Rathke Pouch cyst. He remained only a few minutes.

September 1949 saw many of the world's Neuroradiological Societies meet in Rotterdam for the Second Symposium Neuroradiologicum, the first since the war, under the presidency of Bernard George Ziedses des Plantes who had been a pupil of Schüller in the 1930s. Ziedses des Plantes was at the time Head of the Neurological Clinic at the Municipal Hospital in Rotterdam, and from 1953, the Professor of Radiology at the University of Amsterdam. He invited the professor to submit a paper to the meeting, which Schüller had agreed to do, but he declined to attend, saying that Europe had failed him and the world twice in twenty-five years, and he felt that he could never set foot there again.

This was a momentous occasion; the assembly noted the meeting which had occurred in Antwerp in 1939, with Arthur Schüller at its centre, and declared it to have been the First Symposium Neuroradiologicum. Ziedses des Plantes announced Schüller's inability to be present, referring to him as the "great master"; he proceeded to read Schüller's paper himself and projected a photograph of him on the screen, which evoked a round of applause. The conference then sent a telegram to Schüller on 16 September, with the message:

> The participants send their greetings and thanks to the newly appointed honorary president of the Symposium Neuroradiologicum, hoping he will accept.

These were the men who were writing the history of neuroradiology, and would continue to do so for another generation. From then until the present, the symposium has been the voice of the World Federation of Neuroradiological Societies and, by word and implication, they had gone a long way to confirm Schüller's priority in the field.

Altogether, 1949 had been a good year and it ended well; in December Frank Morgan and John O'Sullivan hosted a dinner for Arthur to celebrate his seventy-fifth birthday at the Athenaeum Club in Melbourne. Morgan, who knew of Schüller's liking for jugged hare, had arranged for this to be the central dish. Served with elaborate ceremony, it brought forth a surprised cry of delight. The professor wore one of his Viennese lounge suits and a wide floppy neck tie, his usual uniform; he did not possess a dinner jacket. He sat at Frank Morgan's right surrounded by eight or ten respectfully dinner-jacketed (on Morgan's instructions) radiologists, neurologists and neurosurgeons. A greatly privileged and somewhat overawed neurosurgical registrar (the author) sat on the left side of the table at the extreme far end. The professor was in good spirits and he spoke of the great medical figures in the Vienna Medical School at the fin de siècle.

In June 1950, the Schüllers bought a house at 2 Mortimer Street, Heidelberg. Situated almost on the crest of a hill, its southern aspect looked out over what was then called the Heidelberg (later Warringal) Cemetery, separated from the boundary by only a road's width. To their home they brought the domestic possessions and furniture which had come to Australia by ship to judge from a pencilled addition to the original immigration documents in 1942. How this came about in the middle of a global war is a mystery; the only certainty is that they were removed from Vienna in 1939 before the war broke out. Presumably they found their way to London and perhaps to the care of Grete Schüller's sister, who had moved to London in 1938.

Their effects included an amount of fine Czech China, some elaborately decorated Austrian furniture in the Biedermeier tradition and a German piano. Frau Schüller gave away the china to the children of her domestic employers as they grew up and married. The piano (R Lipp & Sohn Stuttgart) is in the home of a daughter of the Austen family, in a Victorian rural city. No-one knows the fate of Schüller's violin.

The main room of the house looked eastwards on the hillside, which fell away rapidly, and in the far distance a low blue-grey line of mountains, the Dandenong Ranges. In his last years, Arthur would spend his entire day sitting in the window reading or looking out.

It is tempting to speculate on their decision to buy a house in Heidelberg; Schüller had often spoken about Heidelberg and its university in Germany and, perhaps to draw a long bow, to note also that Heidelberg has been asserted to mean blue hill or mountain. However, there is no support for the idea that *heidel* is an archaic word for blue to be found in the *Oxford-Duden German Dictionary*; in fact, a major survey of German placenames relates it to a dialectal word for "goat". The probable truth is that the location of the house was simply a question of price, suitability of accommodation and accessibility to public transport, as it is for almost all house buyers; they were no more than a five-minute walk from a bus stop which would take them close to the Heidelberg shopping centre and to the city centre of Melbourne. This would have great convenience for his wife, but Arthur Schüller would never have been able to cope with the transport; the house had come too late for that. The building was conveniently entered from the street level of Mortimer Street, but the original front door, which looked over the cemetery across the narrow separating street, required an external flight of stairs, on which Frank Morgan and Arthur Schüller were subsequently photographed.

Around 1950, Arthur's health began to fail, and soon it was obvious that he had developed Parkinson's disease. It was probably this which led to a fall a year or two later, and brought about a fractured femoral neck, which required surgery. He made a remarkable recovery and very soon the characteristic shuffling of his light leather slippers was heard again in the x-ray corridor.

Young doctors at that time recollected many years later that by 1950 a lot of the spark had gone out of Arthur Schüller. He was much less interested in teaching and preferred his own company more often than not. He became more withdrawn and gradually withdrew himself from the life of the hospital which he had previously enjoyed. At this time he was in his mid-seventies and his health was beginning to fail. The early stages of his Parkinsonism, which he clearly must have recognised, along with the major depressive illness that had plagued him years earlier, must have been a heavy burden for him to bear. As all who knew him would attest, there was never even a flicker of complaint or self-pitying.

From then on, he came to the hospital less frequently and ultimately attended only on one day a week. Several years before this, he gave up travelling by public transport and he was brought to the hospital and taken home at the end of the day by their friendly neighbour, Arthur Coombs. This good man was the head of science at a secondary college in a suburb not far distant from the hospital. Mr and Mrs Coombs had sold the Schüllers' house to them in 1950, and they were fortunate that their choice of this house had brought them into contact with the Coombs family, who lived on the other side of the street. They were to remain neighbours and good friends until Grete died (Arthur Coombs had died several years previously). At one time, one of the Combs' teenage children was struggling with Latin at school, and Arthur tutored him on Sunday mornings.

On 9 October 1956, his last day in the hospital, he had four cases for study: a ventriculogram, a carotid angiogram, an air encephalogram and a vertebral angiogram. Having finished the reports in his usual spidery hand, he made his farewells and went home.

Taken by surprise, his colleagues had not arranged a farewell. The journal off-prints and the books which he had brought from Vienna were left for Frank Morgan; they form the nucleus of the Schüller Archive at St Vincent's Hospital. It is not surprising, but sadly regrettable, that the beautifully produced classical monograph on infections involving the temporal bone by his friend and colleague E. G. Mayer disappeared before Frank Morgan could have the collection moved up to his office.

Always reclusive, Arthur Schüller withdrew from social activities but continued to examine problematical skull films which were often sent by courier from the hospital to his home. In the last half of the 1940s, he had often been consulted by Dr Mary Kent-Hughes, radiologist at the Repatriation General Hospital, who brought the films to his office; in the later years they were sent also to his home from that hospital, which was situated only a short distance away in the same suburb.

Friends noted that he spent his days sitting, reading and listening to classical music on the radio; music was his principal joy in life. There were orchestral concerts and other musical activities in Melbourne which were not in any significant degree interrupted by the war years, apart from the absence of some musicians on active service and visiting performers from Europe, but he never moved from their home, even in those early years, to attend one.

Shortly after the end of the war Otto Klemperer, a protégé of Gustav Mahler, conducted a series of concerts with the Melbourne Symphony Orchestra. Schüller was excited by the event but it did not attract him to the Concert Hall; nevertheless, he questioned the registrars about them. He read a lot and his wife brought books from the local municipal library in Heidelberg, but there but there is no record of the borrowings extant.

In his last years, as his Parkinson's disease advanced, the gradual development of chronic cardiac failure added to his burden. His physician, Dr John Horan, previously a medical officer with the Australian Army, had been trapped by combinations of German and Italian forces in the Libyan Mediterranean port of Tobruk where the Australians endured a siege for two years. The only book in his possession was a volume of the poems of the Roman poet Horace, picked up in a second-hand bookshop in Cairo at an earlier stage of the war; this turned him into a Latin scholar. Schüller and Horan enjoyed trading quotations from Horace with competitive banter and good humour; they became close friends through his last twelve months of frequent short admissions to hospital, but he was not forgotten by others.

Letters for him from abroad continued to arrive at the hospital, and these were taken out to 2 Mortimer Street. In late March or early April 1957, he received a visit from the founder of American neuroradiology, Merril Sosman, who had done all the radiology in the clinic of Harvey Cushing, the founder of American neurosurgery. Sosman had been invited by the College of Radiologists of Australasia to tour New Zealand and Australia, reporting on the state of radiology in these countries, spending time in all the major cities. He had been a pupil of Schüller in the 1920s and had remained in contact with him. This must have given Schüller great pleasure.

Arthur Schüller was admitted to hospital for the last time at the beginning of October 1957. He was given a private room on the second floor overlooking the street. Frail now and almost immobile from Parkinson's disease, he was in a state of worsening congestive cardiac failure. No longer interested in trading quotations from Horace with his physician, he slept most of the time, but when wakeful he took pleasure in watching the world go by outside. Deterioration was progressive and it was quickly obvious that he would not leave hospital this time.

The hospital buildings occupy the length of a city block on the north side of Victoria Parade, a wide avenue with a broad central tract of lawn and trees along its length, a tram line between them along its spine, and three lanes of traffic on each side. His room looked out to the south side lined by the Royal Victorian Eye and Ear Hospital, with the tall spires of St Patrick's Cathedral behind, and the major fire station for the city, with its slender Victorian tower, manned in earlier times by an officer of the Metropolitan Fire Brigade on fire-spotting duty. This brigade had no brigadiers and the architecture was not at all militaristic; that was left to the Salvation Army Training School next door with its mock Tudor turrets and bristling battlements. Further to the west comes the Royal Australasian College of Surgeons, set in its own gardens. Between these buildings, in those days, were several large terraced houses of the well-to-do, the largest of which had been converted for St Vincent's Maternity Hospital. In this short section of the boulevard was no commerce, no government office, just a place where a sense of service and quiet civility prevailed despite the six lanes of roaring traffic on one of the busiest streets in the city.

Not quite the Ringstrasse to be sure, but perhaps he saw there the last reminder of his beloved Vienna in the European elms planted there by other nostalgic newcomers to a strange land almost a century before.

Arthur Schüller died on 31 October 1957. The next day, his death was announced nationally on the radio news service of the Australian Broadcasting Commission, adding that he was the only refugee doctor who did not have to undergo an examination to test his competence. Arthur Schüller is buried in Warringal Cemetery in Heidelberg. It was opened in 1855, only twenty years after the informal founding of what became the City of Melbourne. Square in outline and bounded by suburban streets, its sides sitting square to the points of the compass, its small size reflects its origin in an early rural community ten kilometres from what began, unofficially, as the first European settlement in that part of Australia.

Full now, and closed to further burials, it is a sparse and rather desolate place with little green relief, save for a single line of trees along three of its borders, the fourth marked by the endless traffic along Upper Heidelberg Road. The graves run in strict tight parallel lines with little sign of lawn or flowers, and the eye scans a mono-chrome grey scale of stone with narrow pixels of mostly bare earth between. True to the English tradition of the early nineteenth century Georgian era, the graveyard rests on the eastern slope of a hill where the early light of each new day falls first upon the past.

The first grave noted by the visitor entering by the south gate is covered by a plain concrete slab with a vertical headstone faced with marble. It announces quite simply:

In Loving Memory
of
Arthur Schüller
Died 30.10.1957
Margaret Schüller
Died 27.2.1972

Arthur had to wait for the headstone until Grete died. His date of death is incorrect; it should be 31 October. His wife's name is spelt incorrectly. There was no one left to correct the record.

The loving memory lies in the ashes of Auschwitz.

John O'Sullivan died suddenly a few weeks later from a heart attack.

This photo was taken in the early 1950s, probably in the Schüller's garden in Mortimer Street. Arthur is centre with Grete. On the right is Father John O'Connor, parish priest of St John's Heidelberg, and next to him is Frank Morgan. The couple on the left are believed to be the Austens.

Arthur Schüller and Frank Morgan on the front steps of number 2 Mortimer Street, Heidelberg, 1950. The Schüllers bought this house from Mr and Mrs George Coombs in 1950. Morgan was not a regular visitor to the Schüller residence and had little social interaction with him outside of work. This photo, signed by both Arthur Schüller and Frank Morgan was presented to the author at the time of his departing Melbourne for Oxford at the end of his neurosurgical training at St Vincent's Hospital.

This building is 33 Collins Street, where Schüller consulted. This building was owned by the Ryan family, which included a number of well-known Melbourne medical practitioners. It is strongly believed that Schüller was allowed to use the consulting rooms at no cost.

Schüller in the front room of the house in Mortimer St, Heidelberg shortly after moving in (1950). Classical music would have been playing in the background. Normally the blinds would have been closed.

Chapter Ten

A Coda for Grete

Friendship is a kind of elective home, a gift for all of us and an indispensable solace for those who have lost their homeland.

– Fritz Stern
Einstein's German World

It is not common practice for a biography to include a separate treatment for the spouse of his subject, but Grete Schüller has a special claim; she made Arthur's career possible to an unusual degree, and with him, she suffered beyond imagination. She deserves her own retrospective.

Little is known of Grete's early years but she was born in Brno (on 27 November 1886), which suggests the Schüller and Stiassni families may have known each other. Her family were wealthy industrialists in the textile industry.

When Grete finished her secondary schooling, and thus qualified for the *Matura*, which gave her entrance to any German university, she expressed the desire to study pharmacy at the University of Vienna. Vienna had only recently established a faculty of pharmacy, the first in any university worldwide. However, the idea of their daughter plying her trade from a shop front on the high street was considered to be unsuitable for a young lady of her class, and the matter was allowed to drop. She chose to remain at home as a lady of leisure, continuing her studies in music, particularly the piano, and languages.

This was to prove of considerable benefit to Arthur in the years after the First World War, when he began to travel to meetings and universities outside of the German circuit. He had not concentrated on developing skills in the Slavic languages, and Grete became his interpreter, accompanying him wherever he moved. Grete reminisced she first met Arthur at supper in the Sacher Hotel after a performance at the Opera House.

Arthur and Grete were married in 1906, almost certainly in Brno and, according to family tradition which cannot be substantiated, they were married in a Catholic church but, as explained above, this was highly unlikely as they were baptised the year after they were married. If the Stiassni and Schüller families were known to each other before, it was probably through their connections in the textile trade, as well as through the Jewish community.

Shortly after their marriage, the two boys, Franz (1908) and Hans (1909), were born in Vienna. To all observers Arthur and Grete remained a loving and devoted couple.

In Vienna, Arthur's wife would have been a significant social presence, as were the wives of all professors. His private clinical work was conducted in the same apartment building where Arthur and Grete lived, 9 Garnisongasse. Among her own family and equally among Schüller's cousins, she was regarded as a "a bit of a bluestocking" for whom the tasks of rearing children were beyond her lady-like capacity. She was considered to be of a delicate and nervous disposition, and certainly a little eccentric.

The records indicate the Schüllers did not own their apartment at 9 Garnisongasse, which was regarded by members of the family as somewhat downtrodden and below what a professor in the university might aspire to. Grete had a reputation among the family of being very careful with money and could see little value in spending considerable sums entertaining family and friends.

By the time her boys were eight and nine, Arthur was already a busy and distinguished scholar with a heavy teaching and research load on his hands, and little attention given over to social and family life; there was need for a flexible arrangement. We do not know how the necessary arrangements were achieved, but suffice it to say that the boys were for the most part brought up and educated by members of the Stiassni family in Brno during their secondary and tertiary education, with holiday periods spent in Vienna and elsewhere.

That time coincided with the later years of the First World War and the immediate postwar period which were very difficult for the residents of Vienna. Most likely the family considered that the boys were better off out of the city with its food shortages, unstable political situation, overcrowding and the threat of infectious diseases such as cholera and tuberculosis.

Anyway, the arrangement is said to have been a happy one for the boys, who both became very attached to the Stiassni family members while preserving a family attachment to their own parents. Initially the boys lived with Grete's mother, Frederike Stiassni. As the Stiassni family were involved in the textile trades, the boys were educated with a view to management of the family company in due course.

To this end, they did not attend the University of Vienna, as was usually expected of people of the social status to which the Schüllers and Stiassnis had aspired, but rather they went into a technology education stream. Fortunately, Brno possessed a fine technical institute with an emphasis on textile manufacture. It is likely that the decision to educate the boys in Brno was partly influenced by bonds of family, and possibly technical and financial issues, but the decision as described might equally have been applied for the convenience of either Arthur or Grete.

The older son, Hans, lived with Margarete's brother Alfred and his wife Hermine for part of his adolescent years. He was extremely close to Alfred, and was clearly influenced by him in his choice of career in the family textile business. Eventually Hans became a senior manager in the family business, and in his early thirties married Gerda in early 1938. Her maiden name is not certain, but an online genealogy suggests it was Krauss. Their only child, a daughter Eva, was said to have been born possibly on 5 November 1938. Whatever the date of birth, Arthur and Grete never met their granddaughter.

On the strong advice of the eldest brother, Rudolph, Grete's brothers, Alfred and Ernst, were awake early to the political developments and were able to extract themselves from Czechoslovakia, presumably with financial resources, settling in the United States shortly before the Second World War.

Alfred had tried desperately to get both of the Schüller boys to accompany them to the US, and he remained bitterly regretful at not getting Hans and Franz out of the country in time.

Hans was remembered as a competent and hard-working but sociable young man much more like his father than his mother. Lt Stiassni's report repeatedly mentions the support Hans provided to his grandmother Frederike, as the increasing restrictions meant Frederike was less able to care for herself independently.

Franz, on the other hand, was remembered as painfully shy in his late twenties. He stuttered but, surprisingly, had a facility for languages not unlike his mother, and worked in the export department of the family textile business, where his linguistic abilities were put to good use. Apparently he was a good musician, again like his parents, but played the saxophone and possibly the flute. He was regarded as an eccentric, like his mother, with whom he was often compared.

It appears that both the Schüller boys did have considerable contact with their parents, both in Vienna and Brno, and apparently lived in a loving and supportive environment. They were clearly very close to their maternal grandmother and uncles and their families.

⚶

When the Schüllers arrived in Australia, they were in financial difficulties. In 1939 the one-way airfare on KLM from London to Sydney was £160 sterling or 2500 guilders per person (which equates to approximately A$15,500 per ticket in 2018). To secure their exit from Austria, the Schüllers were required to pay the exit tax, as well as a Jewish tax, based on the *Vermögensverzeichnis* document, a list of assets. These documents carefully laid out the financial resources of both the Schüllers and the excessive amounts they were required to hand over to procure their exit from Austria, leaving very little to bring to Australia.

They were not particularly wealthy. They owned a small summer house and an apartment in Brno. The Nazis were assiduous in preventing precious metals, jewels, artwork and cash from departing with the refugees and, of course, the tax was designed to strip away the proceeds from the sale of any land and other items if they had not been already confiscated.

They were allowed to take clothing and other personal items, hence the rather impressive fur coat that Grete can be seen wearing in a photograph taken in Collins Street in 1942. (See Appendix 3.)

It has always been assumed that the Schüllers arrived in Australia with very limited financial resources, and then had to rely on support from a number of sources, especially in the early days. There is mention that they brought with them two cheques in the order of £1250 drawn on the Union Bank of Australia, which in 1939 would have been a considerable amount. Whether they were able to redeem them is another issue, as from all accounts they were financially stressed in those early days.

The only other possible source of funds in the early days may have been a cousin of Arthur's living in Brisbane. After all this time, the above sources of funds must remain speculative. Certainly Arthur's attachment to St Vincent's Hospital brought in a modest income, of which there is no record now, but it seems that it was not a large sum, drawn from the government subsidy which paid for the radiographers.

It would appear that the Schüllers were probably supported by well-wishers for a period after their arrival in Melbourne. Morgan and O'Sullivan were the most likely sources of any support. The Mother Rectress of the Hospital, Mother Gonzaga Considine, may have also assisted through the Mother Rectoress' "special purposes" fund, which would explain the persistent rumours about support from the Hospital.

Whatever the financial arrangement, both Arthur and Grete remained extraordinarily thankful to the Sisters of Charity; after Grete died in 1972 her will disbursed the bulk of the Schüllers estate, $181,054, to the Sisters of Charity of St Vincent's Hospital, a very substantial sum for the times. Of the residuum, modest amounts were allocated to others: $600 to the parish priest of St John's Catholic Church Heidelberg, Father Sheedy; $4,000 each to her nephews Stephen and George Karpeles, and similarly modest amounts to several others.

The most significant financial support in the early years in Melbourne, however, came from Grete's two brothers who had migrated to America from Austria and set up in business there. It is known that for a time the Schüllers received approximately $500 a month from them, but most likely from Alfred. His daughter, Susan Martin, Grete's niece, at the request of her father continued to support the Schüllers in Melbourne for a period after his death. In her will, Grete specifically requested that her niece be informed of her demise.

Because Arthur's income was limited in the early days, the Schüllers' future depended at least partly on Grete finding work. Whatever Grete's family felt about her airs and eccentricities, when the need came, this grand Viennese lady met the challenge by descending into the marketplace and going into domestic service, cooking meals and doing ironing for people in their homes. She was acknowledged as a brilliant cook in her own social milieu, and her first attempt was to secure work with patisseries and cake shops, which were numerous along the Chapel Street shopping strip in Prahran. She had a business card printed and peddled it along the street, but without success.

She turned then to domestic service, which proved to be very successful for many years. She advertised her skills in the small local suburban newspapers and then found interviews in local homes.

One might say that, in fact, it was she who interviewed the people in their homes and she scrutinised them very carefully. A number of the essentials had to be agreed upon, including her complete control over the kitchen; to qualify the household had to contain children.

Over a number of years she collected a large variety of occupations in these households, among the most successful of which were in the home of a prominent businessman, in the home of a test pilot for jet aircraft employed by one of the airlines, a radiologist, an up-market boarding house in South Yarra and a Supreme Court judge. From the outset she made it quite clear that the kitchen was her domain but that she did not do any cleaning or dishwashing after the meal was finished. Grete Schüller was not a scullery maid at all, but she was remembered as an excellent cook.

There was one conspicuous failure, when the judge failed to comply with her edict that the kitchen was not included in the area of his jurisdiction; it appears that a conflict arose in that area and she stormed out. This information was said to have spread rapidly through the legal district in the city, where his Honour had a reputation for irritable behaviour. He continued to occupy his seat on the Bench, but Grete moved on to a chair in another kitchen.

Early on, she increased the range of her services and enjoyed supervising the children at their music practice and their homework when their mothers were absent. After the Schüllers bought their house in Heidelberg, most of her workplaces were chosen in that suburb or those adjacent. These households enjoyed Grete's stories of Vienna and its culture.

Over the years, many of these arrangements were highly successful; she developed genuine friendships with the people of the households, particularly in the years after Arthur died in 1957, and on until she retired from work and, from then, until her death.

From January 1960, she had mounting troubles with her health, most of them related to cerebral vascular disorder. Between January 1960 and February 1972 she was admitted to St Vincent's Hospital on nine occasions. She became increasingly frail; she was forced to give up her work with the families, and she could no longer cope with walking to the shopping strip in Heidelberg looking for discounts. One observer had likened the appearance of this diminutive lady in her long Viennese fur coat as looking like a little old bag lady.

In late 1966, Mr Karger, Grete's nephew, came down from Sydney to see how she was managing. He was dismayed to find that she seemed to be wandering mentally. From this time onwards her health deteriorated steadily. The genuine and fond friendships which developed over the years between her and the employing families became more important; these dear people stepped into the breach and kept an eye on her through those retirement years. They took over her shopping, particularly for food, and in at least two cases bought the food, paid for it, took it to her on a Friday evening and refused to accept the payment which she offered.

The Coombs family, living on the other side of the road, had her constantly in their sights, and on a number of occasions, noting her to be ill, arranged her admission to St Vincent's Hospital. The domiciliary nursing service of St Vincent's Hospital, known as Home Care, visited her regularly as needed. This was an indication of the enduring link between the Schüllers and St Vincent's Hospital; the nearby Austin Hospital would have been far more convenient.

When she was admitted to the hospital for the final time, and presumably on other occasions, she was not admitted to the general ward but rather under the bed card of the medical superintendent, Dr W. M. C. Keane. These beds were generally reserved for members of religious orders, nurses, doctors and other senior hospital staff.

Grete Schüller died in St Vincent's Hospital Melbourne on 27 February 1972. She shares a grave with Arthur in the Warringal Cemetery, Heidelberg.

Grete's piano arrived in Melbourne from Vienna in 1940. She was an accomplished pianist and apparently was very fond of this fine instrument. Mrs Schüller supervised a number of children on this piano. After her death, it passed to the Austen family as Mrs Austen was a great friend of Grete Schüller. Eventually this piano was passed down to the Austen children, and when this photograph was taken in the 1990s, it was in storage in Albury, New South Wales. Previous students of Schüller in Vienna remember him giving his private tutorials at his home, leaning on a piano (presumably this one) on which was placed a light box to show x-rays.

This picture was taken at the home of Alfred Stiassni in Los Angeles, USA in February 1960 by Patricia Austen. Alfred (Grete's brother) is on the left, with his wife in the middle, and the person on the right is the other brother, Ernst Stiassni. (Patricia Austen's husband, a pilot, had come to the Lockheed factory in Burbank just outside Los Angeles to take delivery of a new plane.)

Presumably taken the same day as the photo on page 152. Arthur is clearly showing his age and the effects of Parkinson's Disease.

Grete with her friend and neighbour Patricia Austen.

Chapter Eleven

Obituary

The death of Arthur Schüller was sufficiently noteworthy in Australia to justify a news item on the national radio broadcaster and in the daily newspapers. Frank Morgan wrote a long obituary which was published in the *Medical Journal of Australia* on 16 August 1958. It documented his career, and particularly his time in Australia, and barely hid a deep affection for an old friend.

> From what has been told one may judge that Professor Schüller was a remarkable man. To achieve a fraction of what he did would satisfy the yearning of most men. His genius was adorned by perfect manners and nobility of character; in a lifetime one rarely meets his like.

More so than any other obituary, it reflected on the inherent decency and character of the man. There was more than a passing reference to the events of the war and to the tragic consequences that had devastated Schüller's family and career.

⁂

Although Schüller had not been professionally active for many years, his death did not go unnoticed by major medical journals in North America and the UK. These articles followed the usual format, generally confining themselves to an account of his scientific achievements, which even after many years were still regarded as sufficiently important to justify acknowledging his passing. Several obituaries were published in European journals. One, published in the radiology journal *RöFo* (Advances in the field of x-ray and imaging techniques) in 1958, was an extensive recounting of his academic output, but little else. Erwin Schindler described this article as containing "hypocritical fulsome praise (of the man)… nothing explicit about his tragic fate and no hint of guilt".

The main Austrian medical journals did no better. One indicated he left for political reasons and the other that he emigrated. While only too keen to claim him for their own, there was no mention of the Third Reich, anti-Semitism or the murder of his sons, daughter-in-law and granddaughter.

Europe had failed Arthur Schüller again.

The Schuller's gravestone in the Heidelberg cemetery. Arthur's date of death should be 31.10.1957 and his wife's name is spelt incorrectly. There was no one left to correct the record.

The loving memory lies in the ashes of Auschwitz.

Chapter Twelve

Postscript: The Vienna Medical School

At the start of the twentieth century, the University of Vienna was rightly regarded as one of the most influential and progressive institutions of higher learning in Europe.

It is curious that reflections on the university in the late nineteenth century and before the First World War comment on an undercurrent of anti-Semitism throughout the university. The reality was that within the medical faculty over half of the academic staff were ethnically Jewish and for the most part appear to have been treated equitably. A similar proportion of the medical students were Jewish at a time when Jewish persons made up less than 15 per cent of the population of Vienna and surrounding areas.

The fall of the Austro-Hungarian Empire at the end of the First World War ushered in a period of extraordinary political instability and difficulties for the Viennese. In the immediate aftermath of the war, there were attacks by pan-German nationalists within the university on not only Jewish but also socialist and liberal students. From that time forward anti-Semitism appears to have been relatively common and acknowledged within the university, but again, remarkably, the majority of the academic staff were Jewish.

In the early 1930s, with the rise of fascism in Austria, riots directed against Jewish persons occurred within the university. This came to a head with the murder at the university of the philosopher

Moritz Schlick. It was becoming increasingly obvious that the environment for Jewish academic staff was deteriorating, and from this time onwards there was an increasing stream of defections from the University of Vienna to institutions elsewhere, particularly in the US.

As noted elsewhere, the Anschluss in 1938 had a profound impact on the university. Over 2700 university staff were dismissed, predominantly because of their Jewish heritage. The proportion from the medical faculty may have been higher than the rest of the university, and over half the medical students were also dismissed. This was a calamity for the university; many of its greatest minds, including three Nobel Prize winners, departed, with a calamitous impact on teaching and research. A long-lasting legacy of this disaster was the rise to prominence of leaders in the university based on their allegiance to the ideals of national socialism rather than intellectual or academic rigour.

After the liberation of Vienna by the Russian army in April 1945, the university was one of the first institutions to resume activities. The rush to get the university functioning again after the social dislocation and extensive damage from bombing during the war meant that many of those who had been promoted on the basis of their allegiance to the ideals of national socialism remained in charge. The consequences for the university were long-standing. Unlike many other areas of Austrian life, the university did not go through a period of reflection, much less a robust denazification of its staff. Within a matter of years even those staff who had been identified as having pursued the most egregious of behaviours during the war were able to return to positions in the university. In many cases there was no room for anyone who had been dismissed in 1938 even if they had survived.

To judge by subsequent events in the post-war period, the university retained a culture more in common with the war years. In 1959 the names of Eduard Pernkopf and Fritz Knoll, who had served as university rectors during the war, were added to the plaque memorialising the university's rectors. The death of Ernst Kirchweger, a camp survivor and resistance fighter following an assault sustained during a protest against anti-Semitic statements made by the professor of economic history, Taras Borodajkewycz, had the unintended consequence of focusing the international spotlight on the university and its response to the war years.

❧

It took nearly fifty years for the University of Vienna to come to grips with what had occurred between 1938 and 1945. There were many reasons why eventually the university was forced to confront its past, but one of the most significant was a re-evaluation of Pernkopf's *Atlas of Anatomy*, based on the realisation that dissections of victims executed by the Nazis were used in the preparation of the book.

Throughout the late 1980s and 1990s a number of articles appeared in the medical press, mainly from North America, which induced the University of Vienna to reappraise the circumstances of 1938-45. An article by a Viennese medical professor, Eduard Ernst in the high profile American journal, *Annals of Internal Medicine* in 1995, entitled "A leading medical school seriously damaged: 1938", was the most prominent. This article was based on original work undertaken by the author but also included much valuable data previously only available in German.

The end result of all this agitation was for the university to convene a series of reflective seminars and investigations which brought to light as much of the appalling detail that could be ascertained at that removed period in time. A variety of permanent commemorative installations have been placed throughout the university. An online listing with biographical details of the more than 2700 Jewish affiliates of the university who were dismissed is an ongoing memorial and contains details of Arthur Schüller (http://gedenkbuch.univie.ac.at).

The university now has very clear policies which repudiate the ethos of national socialism.

Appendix 1

Bibliography of Schüller's Papers

Frank Morgan wrote in his obituary of Schüller that he had published over 300 papers. The following list contains 145 papers, far fewer, but to the best of Keith Henderson's knowledge, these are the scholarly works which appeared in what would now be regarded as refereed journals. Schüller was a great publicist and he wrote extensively for a variety of other media, e.g. medical society newsletters which on the whole were informative and educational but invariably re-presented information that had been published in the mainstream literature.

Schüller, A (1900). "Hedonal, ein Hypnoticum der Urethan-Gruppe". *Wien Klin Wochenschr*, 113: 526-28.

Schüller, A (1901). "Eifersuchtswahn bei Frauen". *Jahrbücher für Psychiatrie u. Neurologie*, 20: 292-319.

Schüller, A (1902). "Experimente am Nucleus caudatus des Hundes". *Jahrbücher für Psychiatrie u. Neurologie*, 22, 90.

Schüller, A (1902). "Reizversuche am Nucleus caudatus des Hundes". *Pflüg. Arch. Ges. Physiol.*, 91, 477.

Schüller, A (1903). "Zwei Falle von halbseitigen Kehlkopflähmungen". *Wiener klinische Wochenschrift, xvi*, 982.

Schüller, A (1903). "Zwei Falle von halbseitigen Kehlkopflähmungen". *Wiener klinische Rundschau, xvii*, 568.

Schüller, A (1903). "Dystrophia musculorum progressiva (pseudo hypertrophie) mit Beteiligung d Gesichtsmuskulatur". *Jahrbuch für Psychiatrie Leipzig und Wien, xxiii*, 431-4.

Schüller, A (1903). "Rechtsseitiger Hemiplegie". *Jahrbuch für Psychiatrie Leipzig und Wien, xxiii*, 412.

Schüller, A (1903). "Klinische Beiträge zur Kasuistik der Fehlenkopflähmungen". *Wiener klinische Wochenschrift, xvi*, 1054-61.

Schüller, A (1903). "Ueber die Störung des Flankenganges bei Hemiplegikern". *Neurologische Centralblatt Leipzig, xxii*, 50-2.

Schüller, A (1903). "Beiderseitige totale angeborene Defekt des Musculus Trapezius". *Wiener klinische Wochenschrift, xvi*, 516.

Schüller, A (1903). "Beiderseitige totale angeborene Defekt des Musculus Trapezius". *Jahrbuch für Psychiatrie Leipzig und Wien, xxiii*, 430.

Schüller, A (1903). "Typische Fall einer juvenilen Muskelatrophie einem 30 Jahr Mann". *Wiener klinische Wochenschrift, xvi*, 516.

Schüller, A (1903). "Polymyositis im Kindersalter". *Jahrbuch für Kinderheilkunden Berlin, lviii*, 193-217.

Schüller, A & Robinsohn, L. (1903). "Die typischen Aufnahmen der Schädel-basis". *Wiener klinische Rundschau*.

Schüller, A (1904). "Röntgenologie und Neurologie". *Naturforcher-Versammlung Breslau*.

Schüller, A & Robinsohn, L. (1904). "Die röntgenologische Untersuchung der Schädelbasis". *Wiener klinische Wochenschrift, xviii*, 465-7.

Schüller, A (1905). "Die Schädelbasis im Röntgenbilde". *Archiv und Atlas der Normalen und Pathologische Anatomie.* Hamburg, Germany: Gräfe und Sillem.

Schüller, A (1905). "Hemihypertrophie des Schädels". *Wiener klinische Wochenschrift*, 738.

Schüller, A (1905). "Bitemporale Hemianopsie". *Zeitschrift für Augenheilkunde, XIV*, 362.

Schüller, A (1906). "Experimentelle Pyramidendurchschneidung beim Hunden und Affen". *Wiener klinische Wochenschrift, xix*, 57-62.

Schüller, A (1906). "Ossificationsdefekt des Schädel bei zerebraler Kinderlähmung". *Gesellschaft für innere Medizin und Kinderheilkunde, (18 Januar)*.

Schüller, A (1906). "Ueber atypische Verlaufsformen der Tabes". *Wiener medizinische Wochenschrift, lvi*, 761-817.

Schüller, A (1906). "Ueber atypische Verlaufsformen der Tabes". *Gesellschaft für innere Medizin und Kinderheilkunden*.

Schüller, A (1906). "Fall von Sklerodermie". *Wiener klinische Wochenschrift 1906, xix*, 647.

Schüller, A (1907). "Halisterese des Schädelknockens bei intrakranielle Drucksteigerung". *Verein für Psychiatrie und Neurologie in Wien*, 19 Feb.

Schüller, A (1907). "Turmschädel". *Fotschritte auf dem Gebiete der Röntgenstrahlen, xii*, 354.

Schüller, A (1907). "Ueber Infantilismus". *Wiener medizinische Wochenschrift, lvii*, 625-30.

Schüller, A (1908). "Röntgen Befunde bei Epilepsie". *Wiener klinische Wochenschrift*, 711.

Schüller, A (1908). "Keimdrusen und Nervensystem". *Arbeiten auf den neurologische Institut a. d. Wien Univ 2 Teil*, 208-30.

Schüller, A (1908). "Die Röntgen-Diagnostik der Schädel-und Gehirnkrankheiten". *Wiener medizinische Wochenschrift*.

Schüller, A (1908). "Ueber Röntgen-Untersuchungen bei Krankheiten des Schädels und Gehirns". *Wiener medizinische Wochenschrift, lviii*, 501-6.

Schüller, A (1908). "Ueber psychische Störungen im Kindersalter". *Zeitschrift f. d. Ehrforsch u. Behand. d. Jugendl Schwachsinns Jena, ii*, 206-10.

Schüller, A (1908). "Die röntgenographische Darstellung der diploetichen Venenkanäle des Schädels". *Fortschritte auf dem Gebiete der Röntgenstrahlen., xii*, 232-5.

Schüller, A (1908). "Ein 17 jahr Webergehilfe welcher vor 7 Monaten ein Messerstich gegen die linke Schläfeer halten hat". *Neurologische Centralblatt Leipzig, xxvii*, 88.

Redlich, E, & Schüller, A (1909). "Über Röntgenbefunde am Schädel von Epileptikern". *Fortschritte a. d. Gebiete d. Röntgenstrahlen Hamburg., xiv*, 239-49.

Schüller, A (1909). "Über genuine und symptomatische Migräne". *Wiener medizinische Wochenschrift, lix*, 913-22.

Schüller, A (1909). "Rachitis tarda und Tetanie". *Wiener medizinische Wochenschrift, lix*, 2237-44.

Schüller, A (1909). "Zur Diagnostik der Gehirntumoren". *Medizinische Klinik, v*, 837-9.

Schüller, A (1909). "Röntgenbild des Schädels bei Kleinhirntumoren und Akusticus-tumor". *Wiener klinische Wochenschrift, 1850.*

Schüller, A (1909). "Die Röntgendiagnostik derErkrankungen des Schädels und Gehirns". *Centralblatt f.d.Grenzeb. d. Med. u. Chir. Jena., xii*, 849 and 884.

Schüller, A (1909). "Ein 34 jahriger Tabike mit fast völliger Blindheit und hochgradiger Ataxie". *Gesellschaft für innerer Medizin und Kinderheilkunden, viii*, 212.

Schüller, A (1910). "Röntgendiagnostik der Hirntumoren". *Deutsche Zeitschrift für Nervenheilkunden, xxxviii*, 312-14.

Schüller, A (1910). "Ueber operativ Durchtrennung der Rückenmarkstränge (chordotomie)". *Wiener medizinische Wochenschrift, lx*, 2292-6.

Schüller, A (1911). "Sellare Palliativtrepanation und Punktion des dritten Hirnventrikels". *Wiener medizinische Wochenschrift, lxi*, 182-90.

Schüller, A (1911). "Ueber operativ Durchtrennung der Wurzeln und Stränge des Rückenmarks". *Deutsche Zeitschrift für Nerverheilkunden, xli*. 226-31.

Schüller, A (1911). "Bemerkungen über die sellare Trepanation". Wiener medizinische Wochenschrift, lxi, 3002-5.

Schüller, A (1911). "Zur Röntgen-Diagnose der basalen Impression des Schädels". *Wiener medizinische Wochenschrift, lxi*, 2593-9.

Marschik, M, & Schüller, A (1911-12). "Beitrag zur Röntgendiagnostik der Nebenhöhlenerkrankungen". *Fortschritte a. d. Gebiete d. Röntgen-strahlen Hamburg., xviii*, 237-42.

Schüller, A (1912). *Rontgen-Diagnostik der Erkrankungen des Kopfes*. Wein. Leipzig; Holder. English translation Stocking F (1918). *Roentgen Diagnosis of Diseases of the Head*. St Louis Missouri. Mosby.

Schüller, A (1912). "Die Schädelveränderungen bei intrakranielle Druchsteigerung". *Deutsche Zeitschrift für Nervenheilkunden Leipzig, xiv*, 287-94.

Schlesinger, H & Schüller, A (1913). "Ueber die Kombination von Schädel-tumoren und Hirngeschwülten". *mitt. Gesellschaft für innerer Medizin und Kinderheilkunden, xii*, 120.

Schüller, A (1913). "Beobachtungen von intrakraniellen Verkalkungsherden". *Wiener klinische Wochenschrift, xxvi*, 642.

Schüller, A & Schlesinger, H (1913). "Ueber die Kombination von Schädel-tumoren und Hirngeschwülten". *Wiener medizinische Wochenschrift, lxiii*, 1747.

Schüller, A (1914). "Röntgenologie in ihren Beziehungen zur Neurologie". *Deutsche Zeitschrift f. Nervenheilkunden Leipzig, l*, 188-207.

Schüller, A (1914). "Die chirurgische Behandlung des erhöten Hirndruckes". *Wiener medizinische Wochenschrift, lxiv*, 2288-92.

Schüller, A (1915). "Ueber Gamaschenschmerzen". *Wiener medizinische Wochenschrift, lxv*, 1307-9.

Schüller, A (1915). "Ueber eigenartige Schädeldefekte in Jugenalter." *Fortschritte a. d. Gebiete d. Röntgenstrahlen Hamburg, xxiii*, 12-18.

Schüller, A (1915). "Kriegskasuistiche Mitteilungen". *Militärarzt Wien, xlix*, 323-6.

Schüller, A (1917). "Funktionelle Monoplegie der unteren Extremität akquiriert in Anschluss an Commotio spinalis". *Wiener klinische Wochenschrift, xxx*, 156.

Schüller, A (1917). "Zwei Falle mit lokalisierte Hypertrichose infolge von Affektionen peripher Nerven". *Wiener klinische Wochenschrift, xxx*, 1503.

Schüller, A (1918). "Verkalkungsherd im Gehirn". *Wiener klinische Wochenschrift, xxxi*, 141.

Schüller, A (1918). "Die Kriegsneurosen und das Publikum". *Wiener medizinische Wochenschrift, lxxviii*, 1065-93.

Schüller, A (1919). "Fremdkörper im Gehirn". *Wiener klinische Wochenschrift, xxxi*, 601-4.

Schüller, A (1919). "Ueber nervöse und psychische Störungen im Kindesalter". *Wiener medizinische Wochenschrift, lxix*, 233-9.

Schüller, A (1919). "Ueber nervöse Kinder". *Wiener medizinische Wochenschrift, lxix*, 1537-41.

Schüller, A (1921). "Ueber ein eigenartige Syndrom von Disptuitarismus". *Wiener medizinische Wochenschrift, lxxi*, 510-12.

Schüller, A (1921). "Das Röntgenogramm der Stirnhöhle; ein Hilfsmittel für die Identitats-bestimmung von Schädels". *Monatschrift für Ohrenheilkunde etc. Berlin &Wien, lv*, 1617-20.

Schüller, A (1922). "Zur Röntgendiagnose der intrakraniellen Affectionen mit Hilfe des Dandyschen Verfahrens". *Wiener klinische Wochenschrift, xxxv*, 709-11.

Schüller, A (1924). "Der hypophysäre Typus der sexuelle Impotenz". *Wiener klinische Wochenschrift, xxxvii*, 1041-4.

Schüller, A (1924). "Ueber gunstig verlaufene Epilepsiefälle". *Wiener medizinische Wochenschrift, lxxiv*, 2512-51.

Goldhamer, K., & Schüller, A (1925). "Die Vertikal-und Horizontalebene des Kopfes". *Fortschrift a. d. Gebiete d. Röntgenstrahlen Hamburg, xxxiii*, 183-90.

Schüller, A & Möst, J (1926). "Hypophyse Dysostose". *Wiener medizinische Wochenschrift, lxxvi*, 16.

Schüller, A (1926). "Röntgen ray findings in a series of cases of headache". *Radiology, 7*, 190-200.

Schüller, A (1926). "Dysostosis hypophysaria". *British Journal of Radiology, 31*, 156-8.

Schüller, A (1926). "Sobre deformidades de la cara". *Rev. med. de Barcel., 2sv*, 459-64.

Schüller, A (1926). "Obituary for Rudolf Böhm". *Munchen. med. Wochenschrift, lxxiii*, 2170.

Schüller, A (1926). "The Sella Turcica". *American Journal of Roentgenology N.Y., 16*, 336-340.

Schüller, A (1928). "Röntgendiagnose der Akustikustumoren". *Ergebn. d. med. Strahlenforsch, 3*, 89-95.

Schüller, A (1928). "Die Frakturen des os Petrosum in Röntgenbilde". *Ergebn. d. m. med. Strahlenforsch, 3*, 101-13.

Schüller, A (1928). "Syphilis of the Skull". *Congr. Inter. de Med. Trop. et d'Hyg. Comptes Rendu, 3*, 291-3.

Schüller, A (1928). "Tableau Synoptique des Modifications Radiologique dans les Tumeurs Intracranienne". *Revue Neurologique, 2*, 367.

Schüller, A (1928). "Welche sind die klinischen knöckernen Symptons der generalisierten Xanthomatose?" *Aertzl. Praxis, 6,* 15.

Schüller, A (1928). "Sphenoidale Mucocoele oder zystiche Hypophysentumor?" *Monatschr. für Ohrenh, 66*, 166-72.

Schüller, A (1928). "Bemerkungen über die knöckernen Geschwulste des Schädels". *Wiener medizinische Wochenschrift, 8,* 290-393.

Schüller, A (1928). "Osteoporosis circumscripta del craneo. Aspectos en la autopsia". *Revista oto-neuro-oftalmologica sud-americana Buenos Aires, 7,* 463-9.

Schüller, A (1928). "Medicamentose Therapie der Neurosen". *Wiener medizinische Wochenschrift, 46,* 1108.

Schüller, A (1929). "Röntgen Befunde bei Verletzungen des Kopfes". *Wiener klinische Wochenschrift, xlii,* 560-1.

Schüller, A (1929). "Ueber circumscripte Osteoporose des Schädels". *Medizinische Klinik, xxv,* 631-2.

Schüller, A (1929). "Röntgenuntersuchung des Kopfes bei Epilepsie". *Röntgenpraxis, i,* 742-6.

Schüller, A (1929). "Craniostenosis". *Radiology, 13,* 377-82.

Schüller, A (1930). "Kurze Darstellung der Röntgen-Diagnostik kraniocerebraler Affectionen". *Röntgenpraxis, ii,* 625-6.

Schüller, A (1930). "Ueber eine eigenartige Anomalie ("Pneumokele") des Sphenoids bei Tumoren der Hirnbasis". *Monatschrift f. Öhrenh., lxiv,* 924-8.

Schüller, A (1934). "Kontrastfillung des zervikalen Epiduralraumes". *Fortschritte auf den Gebiete der Röntgenstrahlung, 50,* 149-52.

Schüller, A & Urban, H (1934). "Kraniocerebrale Schemata für die Röntgenographische Lokalization". *Franz Deuticke Leipzig und Wien.*

Schüller, A (1935). "Haematoma durae matris ossificans". *Fortschritte auf den Gebiete der Röntgenstrahlung, 51,* 119-24.

Schüller, A (1935). "Alters-und Geschlechtsbestimmung auf Gründ von Kopfröntgengrammen". *Röntgenpraxis, 7,* 518-20.

Schüller, A (1935). "Über suprasellar Tumoren. Fortschritte auf den Gebiete der Röntgenstrahlung", 48, 1007-8.

Schüller, A (1936). "Röntgenologie und Hypophyse". *Wiener klinische Wochenschrift, 49,* 1259.

Schüller, A (1936). "25 Jahre Chordotomie". *Wiener Med. Wochenschrift, nr 15.*

Schüller, A (1936). "Aus dem offiziellen Protokoll der Gesellschaft der Aerzte in Wien. Zur Diagnose basaler Hirntumoren". *Wiener Klin. Wochenschrift, nr. 15.*

Schüller, A & Nowotny, K (1936). "Subdurale Pneumokephalus bei ethmoidalen Osteom (Status epilepticus letalis nach lumbaler Luftfüllung bei altem Morbus sacer)". *Röntgenpraxis, 8,* 107-8.

Schüller, A (1937). "Funktionelle Röntgensymptomatologie des

Zentralnerven-systems (bei Anwendung von Kontrastfüllungen der zerebrospinalen Liquorraume)". *Fortschritte auf dem Gebiete der Röntgenstrahlen, 56,* 6-7.

Schüller, A (1937). "Röntgenuntersuchung spinaler Erkrankungen." *Radiologische Rundschau, 5,* 263-8.

Schüller, A (1937). "Röntgenfrühdiagnose von Kopfverletzungen". *Fortschritte auf den Gebiete der Röntgenstrahlung, 56,* 193.

Schüller, A (1937)." Obrazy Radiologiczne Roznych Nastepstw urazow czaski". *Polskiego Prezglado Radiologicznego, 12.*

Schüller, A (1937). "Die Regio orbitalis". *Fortschritte auf den Gebiete der der Röntgenstrahlen, 55,* 62-7.

Schüller, A (1937). "V Internationaler Röntgen-Kongress". *Wiener medizinische Wochenschrift, 42.*

Schüller, A (1937). "Über der Röntgendiagnose lokaler Eweiterungen des Wirbelkanals". *Wiener klinische Wochenschrift,* nr. 9.

Schüller, A (1938). "X Ray examination of deformities of the nasopharynx". *Ann. Otol. Rhin.& Laryng,* 109-29, 1929.

Schüller, A (1938). "Die Röntgenographische Darstellung eineger Nervenkänale der Schädelbasis". *Fortschritte auf dem Gebiete der Röntgenstrahlen, 57,* 5-7.

Schüller, A (1938). "Eine Modification der Schüller Aufnahme des Schläfenbeines". *Röntgenpraxis, 10,* 23-36.

Schüller, A & Überall, A (1938). "A case of Neurofibromatosis Recklinghausen combined with lateral spinal meningocoele". *Confinia Neurologica, 1,* 312-17.

Schüller, A (1938.). "Röntgenbefunde bei kindlischer Epilepsie". *Wiener Med. Wochenschrift, 88,* 229-30.

Schüller, A (1939). "Diagnosis of Schüller-Christian Disease". *British Journal of Radiology, 12*, 225-8.

Schüller, A (1939). "Enkephalographische und myelographische Untersuchungen im Fruhstadium cerebrospinaler Erkrankungen". *Radiologia Clinica, 8*, no 2.

Schüller, A (1939). "Über die Technik der Kontrastmittel-Untersuchungen des Zentral-nervensystems". *Radiologia Clinica, 8 nr1*, 31-40.

Schüller, A (1939). "Frontal Decompression suggested as treatment for visual disturbances in Oxycephaly". *Confinia Neurologica, 2*, 303-5.

Schüller, A (1939). "Fehlerquellen der Röntgen diagnose von Nebenhöhlenaffectionen". *Acta Radiologica, 27*, 159-64.

Schüller, A (1940). "Radiography of the Subarachnoid Cisternae at the base of the Brain". *British Journal of Radiology, 13*, 127-9.

Schüller, A (1940). "Frontal Cephalhaematoma". *Brit. J. Rad, 13*, 218-19.

Schüller, A (1940). "X-Ray Symptoms of Intracranial Hypertension". *Confinia Neurologica, 3*, 253-6.

Schüller, A (1940). "The Diagnosis of Basilar Impression". *Radiology, 34*, 214-16.

Schüller, A & Morgan, F (1941). "Arterial Hypertension: A symptom of Intracranial Tumours". *Medical Journal of Australia*, Jan 10, 44.

Schüller, A & Morgan, F (1941). "X-Ray examination in recent head injuries". *Medical Journal of Australia*, May 24: 641.

Schüller, A (1942). "Relief of intractable pain by cordotomy". *Speculum: Journal of the Medical Students Society in the University of Melbourne*, Aug.

Schüller, A (1943). "Note on the identification of skulls by x-ray pictures of the frontal sinuses". *Medical Journal of Australia, 1,* 554-6.

Schüller, A (1946). "Cephalhematoma Deformans". *Surgery, 19,* 651-60.

Schüller, A (1946). "Posterior Cisternal drainage of the Hydrocephalic Third Ventricle (Posterior Third Ventriculostomy)". *Surgery, 24,* 119.

Schüller, A (1949). "Über seltene pathologische Röntgenbilder". *Radiologia Austriaca, 2,* 31-41.

Schüller, A (1950). "A Short Review of Cranial Hyperostosis". *Acta Radiologica, 34,* 361-73.

Appendix 2

Sources

The following were interviewed for this work or provided written requests for information. Many of the St Vincent's clinicians knew Schüller when they were young doctors. This list is based on records of interviews or statements/letters held in the Schüller Archive.

Dr Brian Egan, deputy medical superintendent and historian, St Vincent's Hospital Melbourne

Mr Tom Antonie, surgeon, St Vincent's Hospital Melbourne

Prof. Ivo Vellar, surgeon, historian, St Vincent's Hospital Melbourne

Dr Luke Murphy, gastroenterologist, St Vincent's Hospital Melbourne

Sr Marie-Bernadette Wunsch, RSC

Mrs Patricia Austen, Melbourne

Mrs Susan Martin, San Francisco, USA (daughter of Alfred Stiassni, niece of Grete)

Mrs Margaret Rush (née Arthur), neighbour

Dr John Billings, neurologist, St Vincent's Hospital Melbourne

Dr John Egan, medical officer, St Vincent's Hospital Melbourne

Dr Kevin Harrison, radiologist

Dr Robert Galbally, medical officer, St Vincent's Hospital Melbourne

Dr W Hamilton-Smith, physician, St Vincent's Hospital Melbourne

Dr Yulnna Holyoake, medical officer, St Vincent's Hospital Melbourne

Dr Jeffery Paul, medical offer, St Vincent's Hospital Melbourne

Dr (Bill) WMC Keane, medical superintendent, St Vincent's Hospital Melbourne 1948-85

Ms Judith McCormack, theatre nurse, St Vincent's Hospital Melbourne

Mr Desmond Hurley, surgeon, St Vincent's Hospital Melbourne

Mr Edward Ryan, surgeon, St Vincent's Hospital Melbourne

Dr Neville Rothfield, general practitioner; Grete worked for his family in the late 1940s and 1950s

Dr Lorna Sisely, medical officer, St Vincent's Hospital Melbourne

Dr Herbert Bower, psychiatrist, St Vincent's Hospital Melbourne

Dr John O'Sullivan, son of Dr John O'Sullivan

Prof Sir Peter Morris FRS Oxford

Mr John M Potter FRCS Oxford

Mr Andrew Schuller Oxford

Sister Carmel Slattery, Missionary Sisters of the Sacred Heart, Melbourne

The following institutions provided information for this work.

Melbourne Catholic Diocesan Historical Commission

KLM Amsterdam

Consulate-General of Switzerland, Melbourne

New South Wales Medical Board

Medical Practitioners Board Victoria

Commonwealth Department of Health and Family Services

Johns Hopkins Hospital Archives

Austin and Repatriation Hospital

Religious Sisters of Charity (Sister Maureen Walters)

Australian Archives

University of Melbourne Archive Department

Royal Australasian College of Radiologists

The Royal Australasian College of Surgeons

Archives & Heritage Centre, St Vincent's Hospital Melbourne

Bibliography

Bruno Bettelheim, *Freud's Vienna and Other Essays,*1990, Alfred A Knopf, New York.

Ilsa Barea, *Vienna: Legend and Reality*, 1996, Pimlico Press, London

Elizabeth Barker, *Austria 1918-1972*, 1973, Macmillan Press, London.

George E Berkely, *Vienna and its Jews: The tragedy of success, 1880s-1980s,*1988, Abt Books, Madison Books, Cambridge MA.

Tim Bonyhady, *Good Living Street: The Fortunes of My Viennese Family*, 2011, Allen and Unwin, Australia.

Gordon Brook-Shepherd, The Austrians, *A Thousand Year Odyssey*, 1996, HarperCollins, London.

Barbara Falk, *Caught in a Snare: Hitler's Refugee Academics 1933–1949*, 1998, History Department, University of Melbourne, Melbourne.

Saul Friedlander, *Nazi Germany and the Jews: The Years of Persecution 1933-39*, 1997, Phoenix, London.

Brigitte Hamann, *Hitler's Vienna: A Portrait of the Tyrant as a Young Man*, 1999, Oxford University Press, Oxford.

Alan Janik, Stephen Toulmin,*Wittgenstein's Vienna*, 1973, Simon and Schuster, New York.

Barbara Jelavich, *Modern Austria Empire and Republic 1815-1986*, 1988, Cambridge University Press, New York.

William M Johnson, *The Austrian Mind: An intellectual and Social History 1848-1938*, 1972, University of California Press, Berkeley California.

Malcolm McKeown, 'A History of Radiology in Victoria, 1920-1940'. MD Thesis University of Melbourne.

Frederick Morton, *Thunder at Twilight: Vienna 1913-1914*, 1989, First Da Capo Press, Cambridge MA.

Joseph Roth, *The Radetzky March*, 1995, Penguin Books, London.

Carl E Schorske, *Fin de Siecle Vienna*, 1961, Random House, New York.

Hilde Spiel, *Vienna's Golden Autumn 1866-1938*, 1987, Whidenfeld and Nicholson, London.

Fritz Stern, *Einstein's German World*, 1999, Princeton University Press, Princeton.

Andrew Wheatcroft , *The Habsburgs: Embodying Empire*, 1995, Viking Press, New York.

Robert S Wistrich, *The Jews of Vienna in the Age of Franz Joseph*, 1990,Oxford University Press, Oxford.

AJP Taylor, *The Habsburg Monarchy 1809-1918*, 1948, Hamish Hamilton, London.

AJP Taylor, *The Course of German History*, 1945, Routledge Classics, London.

Magda Whitrow, *Julius Wagner Jauregg 1857-1940*, 1993, Smith-Gordon, London.

Stefan Zwieg, *The World of Yesterday*,1943, University of Nebraska Press, Lincoln NE.

vila-stiassni-90-compr.pdf.

Scholarly Articles

Alper, M G. "Three pioneers in the early history of neuroradiology: the Snyder lecture". *Doc Ophthalmol.* 1999; 98(1): 29-49.

"Arthur Schüller". *Br J Radiol.* 1959 Jan;32(373): 49-50.

Cunningham, J. "Hand-Schüller-Kay-Christian disease and Kay's triad". *N Engl J. Med.* 1970 Jun 4; 282(23): 1325-6.

Jellinger, K A. "A short history of neurosciences in Austria". *J Neural Transm (Vienna).* 2006 Mar; 113(3): 271-82.

Komp, D M. "Historical perspectives of Langerhans cell histiocytosis". *Hematol Oncol Clin North Am.* 1987 Mar; 1(1): 9-21.

Morgan, F. "Arthur Schüller". *Med J Aust.* 1958 Aug 16; 45(7): 241-2.

Robinson, F. "A glimpse at an early neuroradiological landmark; the contribution of Arthur Schüller". *Conn Med.* 1965 Apr; 29: 247-9.

Schindler, E. "Arthur Schüller, father of neuroradiology or: an Austrian scientist's fate". *Wien Klin Wochenschr.* 1998 Feb 27; 110(4-5): 162-6.

Schindler, E. "Arthur Schüller: pioneer of neuroradiology". *Am J Neuroradiol.* 1997 Aug; 18(7): 1297-302.

Angetter, D C. "Anatomical science at University of Vienna 1938-45". *Senate*

"Project of the University of Vienna". *Lancet.* 2000 Apr 22; 355(9213): 1454-7.

Hubenstorf, M. "Anatomical Science in Vienna, 1938-45". *Lancet.* 2000 Apr 22; 355(9213): 1385-6.

Kraus, W, A Gisel, W Platzer. "First hand accounts of events in the laboratory of Prof. Eduard Pernkopf. Interviews by Seyed Hossein Aharinejad and Stephen W Carmichael". *Clin Anat.* 2013 Apr; 26(3): 297-303. doi: 10.1

Kniefacz, K. "A Dark History: Anti-Semitism at the University of Vienna". *The Zine*, Austrian Press and Information Service, November 2015. Available at www.austrianinformaton.org/fall-2015/dark-history

Luberti, R F, A J Brezina, R A Ponticelli, A E Buzzi."Arthur Schüller (1874-1957): A fertile life for radiology with tragic edges". *RAR*, 2012; 76, 62-9.

Fleischner, F. "Dr Arthur Schüller: in memoriam". *Radiology 1958*; 70: 595-6.

O'Day, K, K Hallam, H G Furnell. "John O'Sullivan". *Med J Aust.* 1958 May 31; 45(22): 758-60.

Obituaries

Proceedings of the College of Radiologists of Australia 1959; 3, 55.

Weiner Klinische Wochenschrift 1958; 70, 1055.

Weiner Medizinische Wochenschrift 1957;51/52, 1066.

Radiology 1958; 70, 595-6.

British Medical Journal 1958; March, 525.

Medical Bulletin 1958; June.

Morgan F. Arthur Schüller. *Med J Aust.* 1958 Aug 16;45(7): 241-2.

Australian Newspaper Articles

1. *Adelaide Advertiser* 28.6.41 – announcing registration in NSW.

2. *Argus* Melbourne 12.8.39 – announcing arrival in Australia.

3. *Telegraph* Brisbane 11.8.39 – announcing arrival in Australia.

4. *Courier Mail* Brisbane 30.6.41 – announcing registration in NSW.

5. *Daily Mercury* McKay 12.8.39 – announcing arrival in Australia.

6 & 7. *Courier Mail* Brisbane 11.8.39 + *Northern Miner* 28.8.39 (same text) – announcing arrival in Australia.

8. *Evening News* Rockhampton 30.6.41 – announcing registration in Australia.

9. *Sydney Sun* 27.6.41 – announcing forthcoming registration.

10. *World's News* 15.4.44 – Schüller discussed the role of radiology in forensic medicine.

Appendix 3

Vermoegens Verzeichnis

The Schüllers were required to pay an exit tax and the Jewish tax to obtain clearance to leave Austria. Essentially it amounted to 90 per cent of their disposable wealth. What the official documents don't reveal is the systematic theft of property, jewelry etc. They were left with little of their possessions but did manage to bring out some fine china and Grete's piano, which arrived in Australia in 1942. How they achieved this during the war remains a mystery but it probably came through one of Grete's family living in London at the time of their move.

Grete, 15 July 1938 showing she had:

a. cutlery worth	100 RM
b. half a weekend house in Altenberg N.D worth	90 RM
c. shares worth	22700 RM
d. financial assets	917 – RM
e. pearls worth	4797 and 4650 RM

Card from Finanzamt *erledigt* March 1939. Typed note signed by Grete changing *VermVerzeich* – she paid income tax for first quarter 1939, 755 RM, and other contributions of 4950, 9900,1078, 4200 reducing her *Vermoegen* to 20883 RM.

Hand-written note from Grete 25.11.38 detailing payments of 10000 RM in Sept 38 as tax, and 10.11.38 flight tax 8000 RM.

Arthur, 15 July 1938 showing he had:

a. Half weekend house in Altenberg worth   90 RM

b. Half of Legionaerstrasse 6, Brno as rentable house worth 19104 RM

c. Mortgage half of: 4499 RM at Hypotek

d. ?Loan with Franz Schüller   1128 RM

10.3.39, submitted *VermVerzeich* completed 15.3.39 showing:

a. house values April / now   1174 RM / 270 RM

b. *betreiebsverm*   64715 RM / 19448 RM

c. debts   3377 RM / 3377 RM

d. *gesperrtes vermoeg*   5358 RM / 0 *CredAnstalt* (bonds)

e. *devisen*   2920 RM / 0 Brno (currency)

25.5.39

Exit tax total assets   183975 RM

Jewish tax   26800 RM

Leaving exit tax   39295 RM

payable by 25.6.39

Document valuing:

1. Old x-ray equipment

   library of 120 books

   4000 x-ray plates

   In total: 964 RM

2. Salary   370 RM

    Promotion ring from Franz Joseph   670 RM

    2 paintings   300 RM

    10 Persian rugs   1200 RM

    Violin, viola, cello   1000 RM

    (violin for own use, rest given away)

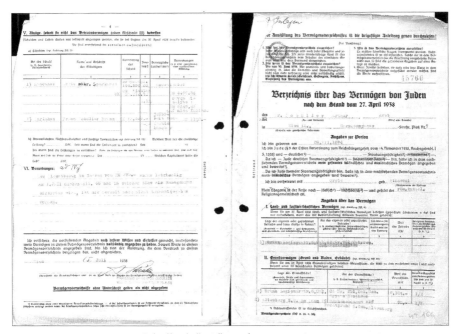

Schüllers's "exit" tax documentation

About the Author

John Keith Henderson, AO, MBBS, FRACS, FRCS
14 January 1923 – 14 July 2017

Keith Henderson was the second-eldest of five children born to Nell and Edgar Henderson, a well-known architect in Perth, Western Australia. He was educated predominantly at Christian Brothers College, St Georges Terrace, Perth, apart from a short time boarding at New Norscia.

He chose medicine as his career, which meant that he did first-year science at the University of Western Australia in 1940 and then came east for the remainder of the course, as Perth was yet to develop a medical school. After first year science in Perth in 1940, despite the offer of entrance into medicine at Melbourne University, he joined the armed forces before orders came through returning him to university, as there was a greater need for doctors.

Keith graduated at the end of 1945, and in April 1946 commenced as a resident medical officer in St Vincent's Hospital, Melbourne. It was during this time he met Pixie Doyle, a nurse at the hospital. Being a Resident Medical Officer meant that he lived in the hospital, where he remained until 29 November 1950 when he walked out the door that morning, married Pixie Doyle a few hours later and sailed to the United Kingdom at 5 pm that afternoon to further his neurosurgical training in the UK.

Their partnership was of an extraordinarily long duration of nearly sixty-five years. They were supremely happy and relied on each other for everything; their devotion to each other was legendary, particularly in more recent years as Pixie's health failed her.

In his second year as a resident medical officer, Keith clerked on the neurosurgery unit under the direction of Frank Morgan, and subsequently he became the neurosurgery registrar (trainee) from 1949 to 1950. Frank Morgan, who had been trained by Sir Hugh Cairns, had set up the first neurosurgical unit in Australia at St Vincent's Hospital. The volume was limited, as was the complexity of the cases. In some ways this was not a good introduction to a life in neurosurgery but he clearly saw something in the discipline that drew him closer.

There were several other events which shaped his future career; arguably the subject of this book was one. We know that Keith had considerable exposure to Schüller as a neurosurgical trainee, and on a number of occasions Keith accompanied Schüller on his Saturday off to the old Sacred Heart Hospital in Moreland to sedate/anaesthetise patients having interventional neurological procedures under Schüller's direction.

Keith also undertook some pathology work, and it is probable that Schüller had something to do with this, as he already had contacts in the pathology department. Schüller also had a limited neurology practice, and I am led to the conclusion that this happy coincidence of a generous man with a vast knowledge who took time to introduce Keith to neuroanatomy, neuroradiology, neurology and neuropathology was considered by both parties time well spent.

Keith and Pixie settled into the UK in early 1951, where he prepared for the FRCS which he duly passed and was awarded a Fellowship of the Royal College of Surgeons of England (FRCS) in 1953. His first position was junior house officer in the neurosurgical unit at the John Radcliffe infirmary in Oxford, and subsequently registrar and finally surgical research officer. Not long after he started, the head of the unit and Nuffield Professor of Surgery in the University of Oxford, Sir Hugh Cairns, an Adelaide graduate and regarded as one of the foremost neurosurgeons in the world, died. His position was taken by Cairns's deputy, Joe Pennybaker, a brilliant young American neurosurgeon who proved to be every bit the leader and clinician Cairns had been.

The time in Oxford was one of the happiest periods of their life. Academically, the department in Oxford was arguably the best place in the world at that time to learn neurosurgery and neurosciences. The associated Institute across the road provided the academic context and the quality of the surgery was without question. The cultural life of Oxford which emphasised intellectual rigor strongly resonated with Keith, and it was one of the fondest memories that he carried throughout his life.

He returned to Melbourne in 1955 to a position as Assistant Neurosurgeon at St Vincent Hospital and received his formal Australian surgical qualification, FRACS, in the same year. His attempts to reproduce the intellectual rigor of Oxford were only partly successful at first. He gradually instituted ward rounds, which included nursing and allied health staff, followed by coffee and St Vincent's scones in the clinic room of St Francis Ward, which became an institution. Colleagues would happen to find themselves in the ward to catch up with Keith and other colleagues just as the coffee was arriving.

Keith knew exactly what he was doing – this was team-building and patient-centred care long before these terms became abused. He loved teaching and found an open market to sell his wares.

He embraced new techniques and introduced them to St Vincent's and his trainees. The transition to the microsurgical era enabled him to further refine his skills and master diverse areas of neurosurgery, from cerebral aneurysms to acoustic neuromas and pituitary tumours, having his own insights into the surgical pathology and the nuances of the surgery itself, all of which he willingly shared.

By his quiet achievement he made St Vincent's a recognised centre for neurosurgery and, together with his contemporaries in other surgical specialties, he helped build the hospital into a surgical powerhouse for treatment and training. In doing so, he acknowledged the essential multidisciplinary nature of neurosurgery and the importance of good relations across the disciplines.

He loved the pathology sessions with his neuropathologist colleague, Ross Anderson, and saw them as vital learning tools. He thrilled at the nuances of neuroradiology from his earliest days where he encountered Arthur Schüller, through the era of neurosurgeons carrying out their own invasive investigations, and then working with Eric Gilford ensuring St Vincent's was at the vanguard of the CT era by becoming one of the first hospitals in Australia to take up the technology.

He was one of the first adopters of functional stereotactic surgery, which required mastery of the radiology as well as of the formidable Riechert frame. He oversaw the transformation of the management of cerebral aneurysms from medical to surgical and steady improvements in the surgical results.

He always had a particular interest in pituitary surgery and took up trans-sphenoidal surgery soon after Jules Hardy brought it back to life in Montreal. His ability to master a new procedure enabled him to achieve results which soon made him a recognised expert Australia wide (with the assistance of Mr P McNeil FRACS).

Finally, there was the legacy of several generations of trainees. From the 1960s onwards, after Keith became head of unit, there was a constant flow of trainees eager to learn from Keith and later his associates in the unit. He taught by example, both within surgery and without. Through it all, he always demonstrated humility, empathy to the plight of the patient and their family, and generosity with his time, whoever needed to be listened to: patient, family, colleague. He never failed to acknowledge the contribution of his co-workers, in particular the ward and theatre nurses who, in their turn, showed him great loyalty.

St Vincent's was enormously important to him, and with the passage of time he became more deeply involved in its affairs. In 1966 he became head of the Neurosurgery Unit and remained so until he retired on his sixty-fifth birthday in January 1988. He served on multiple hospital committees and eventually became chairman of the Senior Medical Staff and close contact with Sister Maureen Walters, the Sister Administrator with whom he developed a close personal and working relationship.

In 1987 Keith was awarded the Order of Australia for services to medicine.

He retired from active neurosurgery on his sixty-fifth birthday and was appointed Chairman, committee for medical graduate education at St Vincent's from 1989 to 1991. His wife's deteriorating health gave him another role to undertake and he essentially became her carer. Apart from enjoying his grandchildren, time spent in his library and writing Arthur Schüller's biography filled his later years.

He is survived by his seven children and twelve grandchildren.

Michael A Henderson is the eldest of Keith and Pixie's children. He received his medical degree from the University of Melbourne and completed his training in General Surgery at St Vincent's Hospital (Fellowship of the Royal Australasian College of Surgeons), followed by a fellowship in surgical oncology at the University of Texas, MD Anderson Cancer Center.

He returned to St Vincent's Hospital as a Surgical Oncologist and the University of Melbourne Department of Surgery, and as consultant surgeon at the Peter MacCallum Cancer Centre. In 2017 he retired as Head of the Breast and Endocrine Surgery Unit at St Vincent's Hospital and continues as Professor of Surgery, University of Melbourne, Head, Melanoma and Skin Service, and Deputy Director Division of Cancer Surgery at the Peter MacCallum Cancer Centre.

Endnotes

1   There is considerable variation in the spelling of Arthur's wife Margarete's name throughout the documents available at the present time. On her gravestone, probably the least reliable source, the spelling is Margaret. On the front page of her Reisepass (German passport) the spelling is Margarethe but on the inside page the spelling is Margarete. Interestingly, her husband on his entry papers to Australia calls her Grete. This is apparently the name she was known by and will be used in this text.

2   Fifteen years later when the author returned from Oxford, Schüller's first words were to ask about Joe Pennybacker.

3   Sunderland, later Sir Sydney, was to become Dean of the Faculty of Medicine at his university. He was a more than able administrator and remained an active researcher throughout his career. His monograph Nerve and Nerve Injuries 1968 drew heavily on his clinical and research activities and was widely admired.

4   Seventy years later both men were honoured by the issue of a commemorative postage stamp.

5   Ross Jones. *Humanity's Mirror. 150 years of anatomy in Melbourne.* 2007.

6   Julian Smith was something of a polymath, with wider interests than medicine. He was regarded as an extra-ordinarily gifted surgeon and an early proponent of direct blood transfusion, and collaborated with early haematologists in the care of their patients; he invented the roller pump to facilitate the transfer from donor to the recipient presaging the era of extra-corporeal bypass.

7 Charles' report was based on interviews with surviving friends of the family including at least one who had been in the camps with the Schullers. Given the circumstances it is not surprisingly that some of their recollections were a little vague and in several places do not completely agree with formal records of movement and dates of death of camp internees currently available.

8 Other sources suggest that Gerda was pregnant at that time, but there is considerable conjecture about this statement as Eva was probably born in late 1938. Lt Stiassni reports that Frederike spent time with Eva and Gerda in 1941.

9 Eva was probably aged three years at this time.

10 Gerda and Eva were transported on 01 03 1942, Hans? 02 04 1942 and Franz on 20 02 1942, all to Theresienstadt (Arulsen Archives Theresienstadt Ghetto Transportation cards).

11 His original transportation document indicates Franz was deported from Brno on 20 11 1942 (Arulsen Archives Theres·enstadt Ghetto Transportation cards).

12 Hans arrived in Theresienstadt on ?02 11 1942 and was transported to Auschwitz on 15 12 1943 (Arulsen Archives Theresienstadt Ghetto Transportation cards).

13 When this young woman moved on, he wrote her a gracious letter of appreciation and congratulations which she kept for more than fifty years until she gave it to the author after a chance meeting.